Cambridge Elements ≡

Elements in Business Strategy
edited by
J.-C. Spender
Kozminski University

STRATEGY-MAKING AND ORGANIZATIONAL EVOLUTION

A Managerial Agency Perspective

Robert A. Burgelman
Stanford Graduate School of Business

Yuliya Snihur
TBS Education

Llewellyn D. W. Thomas
IESE Business School

CAMBRIDGE
UNIVERSITY PRESS

Shaftesbury Road, Cambridge CB2 8EA, United Kingdom

One Liberty Plaza, 20th Floor, New York, NY 10006, USA

477 Williamstown Road, Port Melbourne, VIC 3207, Australia

314–321, 3rd Floor, Plot 3, Splendor Forum, Jasola District Centre,
New Delhi – 110025, India

103 Penang Road, #05–06/07, Visioncrest Commercial, Singapore 238467

Cambridge University Press is part of Cambridge University Press & Assessment,
a department of the University of Cambridge.

We share the University's mission to contribute to society through the pursuit of
education, learning and research at the highest international levels of excellence.

www.cambridge.org
Information on this title: www.cambridge.org/9781108983983

DOI: 10.1017/9781108987684

First published 2023

A catalogue record for this publication is available from the British Library.

ISBN 978-1-108-98398-3 Paperback
ISSN 2515-0693 (online)
ISSN 2515-0685 (print)

Strategy-Making and Organizational Evolution

A Managerial Agency Perspective

Elements in Business Strategy

DOI: 10.1017/9781108987684
First published online: March 2023

Robert A. Burgelman
Stanford Graduate School of Business

Yuliya Snihur
TBS Education

Llewellyn D. W. Thomas
IESE Business School

Author for correspondence: Yuliya Snihur, y.snihur@tbs-education.fr

Abstract: This Element presents several frameworks of strategy-making that serve to analyze organizational evolution processes within and beyond the firm. These frameworks form an integrated evolutionary ecological lens to examine the dynamics of strategy-making in organizational evolution. They highlight the role of the internal selection environment for analyzing processes and practices at various managerial levels (top, middle, and operational) within the organization. The Element also explains the role of the CEO in maintaining and updating the internal selection environment and contributing to organizational evolution, as well as making fundamental decisions about organizational splits of the firm's business models as an ecosystem evolves.

Keywords: organizational evolution, strategy-making, CEO strategic leadership, managerial agency, frameworks for strategic management

ISBNs: 9781108983983 (PB), 9781108987684 (OC)
ISSNs: 2515-0693 (online), 2515-0685 (print)

Contents

Preface

This Element did not emerge fully formed but instead represents decades of scholarship. The intellectual journey behind this Element started at Antwerp University (Belgium) with undergraduate research on optimal firm size in the late 1960s (Burgelman, 1969). This integrated insights from Chandler's (1962) historical research on the relationships between strategy and structure in diversifying US corporations, Penrose's (1959) economic analysis of the role of internal entrepreneurship in the growth of the firm, and Ansoff's (1965) (then) radically new analytical treatment of corporate strategy. The integration of these insights inspired the proposition that firm size at any given moment in time had to be considered as the outcome of a process of dynamically adjusting strategy and structure. This process integrates the internal impulse to grow (as argued by Penrose) and the organization-level response to externally emerging growth opportunities (as suggested by Chandler) and can be optimally guided by the components of corporate strategy (as predicated by Ansoff). Shortly thereafter, Bower's (1970) field study, which documented and conceptualized the process of strategic capital investment in a large diversified chemical firm in terms of the contributions of different levels of management to the definition, impetus, and structural context parts of the resource allocation process, fundamentally shaped thinking about the interplay between organization theory and business policy.[1]

The journey continued at Columbia University with Burgelman's dissertation research on internal corporate venturing (ICV) in a diversified major science-based chemical firm (Burgelman, 1980). This work was initially inspired by the applied anthropological research methods of Leonard Sayles (1965) focused on documenting different types of managerial behaviors and their interrelationships in complex organizations. Initial efforts to map all the detailed behavioral data obtained through in-depth field research during 1976–1977 concerning activities of different levels of management involved in ICV onto Bower's process model of strategic capital investment failed to accommodate all the documented managerial activities. Eventually the anomaly was resolved by extending the process model to encompass *strategic context determination* as a critical aspect. Today this model is known in the literature as the Bower–Burgelman (B–B) process model (Mintzberg et al., 1998).

The findings of the ICV process also produced an anomaly in relation to Chandler's fundamental proposition that "structure follows strategy." The ICV

---

[1] As a junior faculty member at Antwerp University, Burgelman reviewed Bower's book for the *Economisch en Sociaal Tijdschrift* in 1971, and subsequently collaborated with senior professor Andre van Cauwenbergh on integrating business policy and organization theory for a new course in the Faculty of Applied Economics.

research found that the creation of a New Venture Division was, at least in part, a response to the company already having several new venture initiatives dispersed in different divisions and the corporate R&D function before top management had articulated a deliberate corporate-level diversification strategy (Burgelman, 1985). This finding indicated the existence of autonomous strategic initiatives (not driven by the existing corporate strategy) in parallel with induced strategic initiatives (driven by the existing corporate strategy) (Burgelman, 1983c).

Continuing the journey at New York University (1978–1981) and then at Stanford University (from 1981 on), the discovery of autonomous strategic initiatives related to ICV suggested a reconceptualization of the ICV process in terms of "corporate entrepreneurship" and inspired the development of a theoretical framework integrating corporate entrepreneurship and strategic management (Burgelman, 1983a). This framework also made an early connection to work on complexity theory and the shift from the physics of "being" to the physics of "becoming" by Nobel Prize winner in chemistry Ilya Prigogine (1980). Decades later, this would form part of the conceptual foundation of strategy-making shaping the process of organizational evolution extended with the coauthors of this Element. An additional finding of the ICV research concerned the multilevel interplays between action and cognition, which suggest that the strategy-making process associated with corporate innovation involves a social learning process in which managers at middle and senior levels interpret (through cognition) the strategic implications of the actions of lower-level managers, which then drives their own actions, culminating in top management's support for a change in the corporate strategy (Burgelman, 1984, 1988). This early conceptualization of action-cognition interplays in organizations would not gain traction in the strategic management literature until much later.

The framework of induced and autonomous strategy processes could also be related to the variation–selection–retention paradigm of cultural evolutionary theory (Campbell, 1965; Weick, 1979). This intersected with some of the theoretical and empirical implications of the field of organizational ecology in organization theory, suggesting the possibility for a rapprochement between strategy and ecology (Burgelman & Singh, 1987). During the same period (1986–1990), efforts to apply simulation techniques to the induced/autonomous strategy-making processes resulted in CORPSTRAT: a discrete event simulation model of the intraorganizational ecology of strategy-making for studying individual and organizational decision-making and related processes, such as managerial risk behavior, performance, and survival (Burgelman & Mittman, 1994). Simulations have since become an important methodological addition to studying organizational evolution (Levinthal, 2021).

Starting in late 1988, further development of the internal ecology of strategy-making framework, which viewed large and complex organizations as ecological systems, became possible with longitudinal field research at Intel Corporation (Burgelman, 1991). The study of Intel's transformation from a semiconductor memory company to a microprocessor company resulted in the development of the "Dynamic Forces Driving Firm Evolution" framework (Burgelman, 1994). This framework helped highlight the powerful inertial forces associated with distinctive competence and the crucial importance of an organization's internal selection environment in coping with the external selection environment. A surprising insight of this paper was that strategic action – related to resource allocation – that diverges from the no-longer-adaptive corporate strategy but is compatible with changes in the external selection environment has survival value; in contrast, strategic action that is tightly aligned with the stated but no-longer-adaptive strategy does not. This framework also served to develop a practitioner-oriented framework for addressing "strategic inflection points" – periods of crisis in the evolution of companies – that are signaled by "strategic dissonance" emerging among the company's senior and middle management in response to structural changes in the firm's business ecosystem (Burgelman & Grove, 1996).

Tracking Andy Grove's tenure as Intel's CEO during the rapid growth of the PC ecosystem in 1988–1998 revealed the potential dangers of the CEO "vectoring" the corporate strategy when a company has the opportunity to singularly dominate its business ecosystem. It also identified the novel phenomenon of "co-evolutionary lock-in" (Burgelman, 2002a). The conceptual frameworks derived from the Intel research could be combined into an evolutionary lens on strategy-making (Burgelman, 2002b). Finally, the research lens of the internal ecology of strategy-making was used to examine various types of nonlinear strategic dynamics that Intel had faced throughout its evolution, producing insights that defined the role of the CEO in terms of "let chaos reign, then rein in chaos – repeatedly" to manage strategic dynamics for corporate longevity (Burgelman & Grove, 2007).

The research stream on Intel's transformations stimulated further research interest by Burgelman in corporate longevity in turbulent environments. This new research stream focused on Hewlett-Packard (HP), a company founded in Stanford University's backyard that had been able to transform itself multiple times by the mid-1990s. The research identified successive CEOs as a seldom-studied unit of observation, and John Young, Joan Platt (Lew Platt's widow, who provided interesting and poignant insights into Lew's tenure as CEO), Carly Fiorina, Mark Hurd, Léo Apotheker, and Meg Whitman made time to participate in interviews and provide the CEO perspectives that augment the foundation for developing the theory of strategy-making and organizational evolution (Burgelman et al., 2017). Beyond using the frameworks derived from the previous Intel research to compare the strategic leadership of successive HP CEOs, this research generated a novel, inductively derived conceptual framework for explaining why CEO Meg Whitman decided to split HP into two new, independent companies in 2014.

In fall 2016, Yuliya Snihur visited Stanford and engaged in discussions about business-model innovation and ecosystem disruption with Burgelman. These interactions, also involving Llewellyn Thomas, inspired collaborative research related to ecosystem-level dynamics associated with business-model innovation at the firm level (Snihur et al., 2018). The initial collaboration continued with further joint study of the dynamics relating to organizational strategy-making, business-model changes, and ecosystem evolution. In particular, Snihur and Thomas took the initiative in developing large-scale longitudinal archival databases to study the extent to which the two novel conceptual frameworks derived from the HP field research could be corroborated. They also engaged in extensive literature research to link these frameworks to received knowledge and help to clarify the extent to which the frameworks filled gaps in the literature (Burgelman et al., 2022a, 2022b).

As well as representing a fascinating intellectual journey, underpinning this Element is a bridging of history and reductionism. The ICV dissertation research (Burgelman, 1983a) was among the first to apply Glaser and Strauss's (1967) method of "grounded theorizing" in the field of strategic management. Grounded theorizing is an inductive method that uses rich comparative field data to inductively derive novel theoretical concepts and frameworks to attain deeper understanding of substantive phenomena. As Spender and Kraaijenbrink (2011: 52) explain, "frameworks identify the relevant variables and the questions that the user must answer in order to develop conclusions." This involves iterative and comparative work, examining different types of data, and moving back and forth between emerging theory and the phenomenon under study. This back-and-forth movement is needed to abstract generalizable and theoretically relevant insights from empirical cases under examination.

Glaser and Strauss (1967: 33–34) made an important and often overlooked distinction between *substantive* and *formal* grounded theory. They consider both as "middle range" – falling between minor working hypotheses and grand theories. They view substantive theory as "a strategic link in the formulation and generation of grounded formal theory. We believe that although formal theory can be generated directly from data, it is most desirable, and usually necessary, to start the formal theory from a substantive one" (Glaser & Strauss, 1967: 79). Developing formal theory without first developing a substantive theory grounded in research of a particular substantive phenomenon runs an important risk: "When the theory is very abstract, it becomes hard to see how it came from the data of the study, since the formal theory now renders the data without a substantive theory intervening" (Glaser & Strauss, 1967: 81). Glaser and Strauss also point out that: "Our strategy of comparative analysis for generating theory puts a high emphasis on *theory as a process*; that is theory as an ever-developing entity, not as a perfected product" (1967: 32; italics in the original). Hence, the methodology of grounded theorizing offers the opportunity for both exerting disciplined creativity and enjoying the associated intellectual pleasure of discovery – but, at the same time, it reminds the researcher that their theory-generation effort is only a step along the road toward additional, cumulative knowledge development that will lead to future modification and reformulation. In this Element, we endeavor to integrate models of strategy-making of different substantive areas into a more formal theory of strategy-making in organizational evolution.

The original grounded theorizing method emphasized the comparative dimension of research at the expense of the temporal one. The longitudinal research on the evolution of Intel and HP made it possible to introduce a stronger temporal perspective into grounded theorizing, which helped bridge historical narratives and reductionist quantitative models (Burgelman, 2011). This longitudinal grounded theorizing method could be situated between the historian's "particular generalization," characterized by complex and nonlinear causation, and the reductionist's "general particularization," characterized by statistically based models, mathematical axiom-based models, or simulations (Gaddis, 2002). This is presented in Table 1. In this Element, we capitalize on using the longitudinal dimension of grounded substantive research to develop our more formal theory of strategy-making and organizational evolution.

Inductively derived from small samples, the conceptual frameworks originating from longitudinal grounded theorizing naturally face questions about their external validity and generalizability. To address these concerns, we complemented the longitudinal grounded theorizing method, which relies on interpretative field data analysis, with realist historical research based on archival data (Vaara & Lamberg, 2016). In this combinatory research method, interpretative field data analysis involves interpreting the meaning of statements and actions based on qualitative data collected through interviews. Realist historical research involves the collection of extensive longitudinal archival data to examine whether the emerging theoretical framework can be independently corroborated through data sources other than interviews and researchers' own observations. This novel combinatory method ensures the robustness of derived frameworks

Table 1 The bridging role of longitudinal qualitative research in theory development

History: Particular generalization	←→	Longitudinal qualitative research	←→	Reductionism: General particularization
Particular		Specific		General
Concrete		Substantive		Abstract
Experiential		Suggestive		Nonexperiential
Narratives		Conceptual frameworks (boxes-and-arrows charts)		Statistical and mathematical models

Source: Burgelman (2011: 598).

and can help increase trustworthiness. We used it to examine the extent to which the framework for corporate split, a novel form of divestiture and portfolio reconfiguration derived from the HP study (Burgelman et al., 2022), as well as the framework of successive CEOs' strategic leadership of HP's continued organizational adaptation (Burgelman et al., 2022a), could be corroborated.

1 Introduction

In this Element, we consolidate an evolutionary theory of organizational strategy-making based on scholarly contributions over the past fifty years.[2] We analyze the firm through the lens of intraorganizational ecology, and showcase specific tools developed to clarify the role of *strategy-making*, a process involving the thinking and action of key managers and employees across the vertical and horizontal levels within the organization, in shaping *organizational evolution*. Organizational evolution refers to the unpredictable but potentially manageable process of long-term organizational adaptation in response to changing external and internal contexts (cf. Tsoukas & Chia, 2002). It concerns the way complex systems of strategy-making change a company's business model(s)[3] and institutional identity as it attempts to survive the relentless forces of Schumpeterian creative destruction – and it implies, importantly, that organizations should be studied as continuously evolving (Weick & Quinn, 1999).

---

[2] We rely on sociology-based evolutionary theories rather than on economics-based ones, such as Nelson and Winter (1982), who view organizational routines as the key elements – like genes – resulting from and driving organizational evolution.

[3] Consistent with others (Massa et al., 2017; Snihur & Zott, 2020; Zott et al., 2011), we define a *business model* as a system of interconnected activities performed by a focal firm (and often also by users and partners) that create value, and a profit logic that captures at least some of that value.

Sometimes, insights derived from new and somewhat unusual research unexpectedly fit most readily with theory that lies beyond received wisdom in the field. In this case, the link is with the organizational learning and organizational ecology perspectives of evolutionary organization theory, as well as insights from complexity theory. The organizational learning perspective of evolutionary organization theory focuses on how organizations, in trying to adapt, search for and use information – that is, how they proactively manage their fit with the external selection environment through internal processes of variation, selection, and retention. While organizational learning does not necessarily lead to organizational adaptation – organizations, composed of people, can learn the wrong lessons! – this perspective leaves room for cognitive managerial processes and knowledge development that is purposeful, even if only myopically so, in driving organizational change. Strategy-making as an adaptive organizational capability is one manifestation of evolutionary organization theory.

The organizational ecology perspective (Hannan & Freeman, 1977, 1984), on the other hand, suggests that organizational change must be understood at the level of entire populations of similar organizations, and as the result of replacement and selection rather than adaptation. Incumbent companies fail in the face of environmental change because inertia prevents them from adapting and they are replaced with newcomers that do different things, or the same things differently ("better," in the eyes of most customers). Such a logic is visible, for instance, in the recent studies on disruptive innovation that illustrate how new business models displace incumbents (Snihur et al., 2018). Organizational ecology, however, does not focus on the role of strategy-making in the entities that make up the populations of study, and leaves little room for explanations of organizational adaptation based on strategy-making.

Established companies are perennially subject to the selection force of the external environment (e.g., Burgelman & Grove, 2007) – and many do, in fact, succumb to it in the long run. But established companies have also gained the opportunity to substitute, to some extent, internal selection for external selection. This is the central idea of the internal ecology model of strategy-making, anchored in the processes determining the functioning of the internal selection environment. An established company can be viewed as an ecological system in its own right, and its survival and continued success depend on the functioning of this internal ecology during the complex environmental changes that can unfold over an organizational lifetime.

This Element is based on the premise that there need not be a fundamental opposition between the ecological and strategic management perspectives, and that a fruitful integration of these ideas is possible in some ways. To pursue this aim, we use the variation–selection–retention framework of cultural evolutionary theory (Aldrich, 1979; Campbell, 1965; Weick, 1979), which has previously been applied to strategy-making by Western (Burgelman, 1983c) as well as Japanese (Kagono et al., 1985) scholars. We extend earlier work by addressing research questions motivated by the evolutionary perspective, always keeping in mind the various ways in which strategy-making manifests. Some of these concern strategy content and process: How does the content of an organization's strategy come about, and how does it evolve? How do strategy-making processes take shape over time? Of particular interest are questions concerning some of the connections between strategy-making processes and different forms of organizational change and adaptation: What, if any, is the link between strategy-making and inertia? Which sorts of strategy-making processes lead to major strategic change that is survival enhancing? And what is the role of strategy-making in organizational evolution?

This Element views an organization as an ecology of strategic initiatives that emerge – through strategy-making – in patterned ways and compete for limited resources to increase their relative importance within the organization. Strategy results, in part, from selection and retention operating on internal variation associated with strategic initiatives. Variation comes about, in part, as the result of individual strategists seeking to express their technical and social skills, and advance their careers, through the pursuit of different types of strategic initiatives and business-model experiments. Selection works through administrative, cognitive, and cultural mechanisms regulating the allocation of attention and resources to different areas of strategic initiative. Retention takes the form of organization-level learning and distinctive competence, embodied in various ways – organizational goal definition, delineation of domain and business model(s), and shared views of organizational identity. In this perspective, the focus of analysis is managerial activities associated with strategic initiatives, rather than individuals per se (Cohen & Machalek, 1988). Our analysis suggests how opposing ideas concerning the expected consequences of major strategic change – that is, organizational inertia or different potential modes of adaptation (Burgelman, 1991; Hannan & Freeman, 1984; Tushman & Romanelli, 1985) – can possibly be reconciled by connecting strategy-making from different levels within the organization through simultaneous and sequential process models.

Our analysis also suggests that the expected consequences of major strategic change can also be reconciled by connecting strategy-making and intraorganizational ecology with the business ecosystem (or interorganizational ecology) and the related dynamics. A business ecosystem is "the broader economic context which a focal firm must monitor and react to" (Thomas & Autio, 2020: 13) and consists of the "economic community of interacting actors that all affect each other through their activities, considering all relevant actors beyond the boundaries of a single industry" (Jacobides et al., 2018: 3). While current ecosystem literature has focused primarily on technological interdependencies (e.g., Adner & Kapoor, 2010; Jacobides et al., 2018), there is much less research that has considered the interplay between the firm-level strategy-making and the business ecosystem (although see Helfat & Raubitschek, 2018; Schreieck et al., 2021). In starting to unpack this interplay we move beyond the strategy-making at different levels within the organization to also include the fundamental role of the CEO in shaping and responding to business ecosystem evolution.

We highlight the managerial relevance of the conceptual frameworks discussed in the sections that follow and their deeper implications for understanding the emergence of novelty and pathways to maintain continuous innovation in evolving organizations and business ecosystems. Together, these conceptual tools emphasize the key role of strategy-making processes in organizations involving the strategic leadership activities of multiple levels of management. We illustrate the relationship between these tools in Figure 1, which is discussed in more depth in Section 4. This figure connects the evolving business ecosystem (top arrow), the internal ecology (bottom arrow), and the strategy-making of the CEO (successive CEO tenures in the middle). Although not included in this figure explicitly, CEO strategic leadership is tightly connected to the strategizing and actions of organizational managers and executives at other levels of the organization that together contribute to the maintenance (or change) of the company's business model(s) and its long-term evolvability.

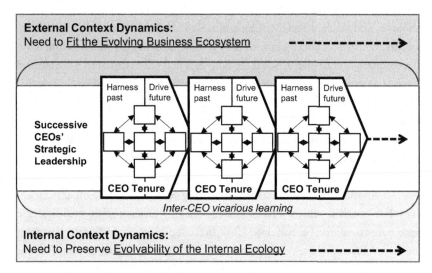

Figure 1 Framework of successive CEO strategic leadership
Source: Adapted from Burgelman et al. (2017: 357).

The Element makes three contributions. First, we highlight the usefulness of complementing received organizational evolutionary theories (e.g., Levinthal, 2021; Nelson & Winter, 1982) with an evolutionary ecological process lens to better understand the dynamics of strategy-making in organizations and ensuing organizational evolution. This internal ecology perspective on strategy-making emphasizes the role of the internal selection environment for analyzing and describing processes and practices at various managerial levels (top, middle, and operational) within the organization (see Section 2). Second, we summarize several frameworks of strategy-making developed during the past fifty years, which are relevant to analyze organizational evolution processes within and beyond the firm (Sections 2, 3, and 4). These frameworks help to understand, analyze, and manage a variety of substantive corporate strategy-making situations and challenges (such as product or business-model innovation, renewal, split, and disruption). Third, we confirm and explain further CEO strategic leadership in organizational evolution and the related strategy-making processes (Section 4). We discuss the role of the CEO in maintaining and updating the internal selection environment and contributing to organizational evolution, as well as making fundamental decisions about organizational splits during ecosystem bifurcations. Together, these insights strengthen the development of an evolutionary understanding of organizational strategy-making (Section 5 and Epilogue).

2 The Internal Ecology of Strategy-Making

Viewed in narrow, purely technical terms, strategy involves planning the use of resources and the deployment of capabilities to achieve objectives and prevail in competition. A broader organizational view includes the rational determination of a company's vital interests and the purposes that are essential to its continued survival as an institution. In this view, strategy is concerned with the external and internal forces that have the potential to materially affect a company's destiny (Burgelman, 2002a).

Adopting an evolutionary theoretical perspective to study how strategy comes about and what role it plays in shaping a company's destiny focuses on *strategy-making* as an organizational (not only individual) process[4] and raises several important questions that are not readily contemplated by other perspectives. For instance, which sorts of strategy-making processes produce strategic change that is survival enhancing? How do strategy process and strategy content coevolve? What are the consequences of periods of extraordinary success for

---

[4] Henry Mintzberg (1978) was among the first to pay systematic attention to strategy as an organizational process. Also see Paret (1986).

strategy-making as an adaptive organizational capability? And what is the link between strategy-making and organizational inertia? These questions extend the frontier of the field of strategic management and can be addressed with the help of the conceptual frameworks that evolutionary organization theory provides. The fundamental research questions raised here extend the dynamic perspective on strategy introduced by Chandler and Penrose, and complement the issues raised by Rumelt et al. (1994) as the defining questions of the field of strategy.

This section introduces three interrelated conceptual tools rooted in evolutionary organization theory (the third is discussed in more depth in Section 3). It is organized as follows. Section 2.1 discusses key processes that constitute the analytical core of evolutionary organization theory and two of its approaches – organizational ecology and organizational learning – that are especially useful for studying strategy-making, and briefly introduces three conceptual tools that, together, serve as an evolutionary research lens for studying the role of strategy-making in firm evolution. Section 2.2 offers detailed discussions of the three tools. Section 2.3 summarizes the implications of an evolutionary perspective for the role of strategy-making in organizations.

2.1 Evolutionary Processes: Variation, Selection, and Retention

Variation, selection, and retention are the key processes of evolutionary organization theory. According to Aldrich (1999), *variation* "is a departure from routine or tradition, and may be intentional or blind." Intentional variations result from the deliberate attempts of people or organizations to generate alternative opportunities and seek solutions to problems. Blind variations, on the other hand, "result from accidents, chance, luck, conflict, malfeasance, creative exploration, and so forth." Aldrich defines *selection* as generated by forces "that differentially select or selectively eliminate certain types of variations ." Selection occurs within organizations as well as at the organization and population (e.g., ecosystem) levels. *Retention* "occurs when selected variations are preserved, duplicated, or otherwise reproduced so that the selected activities are repeated on future occasions or the selected structures appear again in future generations." Finally, *competition* is defined as a struggle for scarce resources that occurs between strategic initiatives within organizations, between organizations, and between populations.

These are generic processes that are not necessarily biological in nature (e.g., Boyd & Richerson, 1985; Dawkins, 1986) and can be fruitfully applied to organizational evolution. The central axiom of evolutionary organization theory is that these key processes are necessary and sufficient for organizations to emerge and evolve. They occur simultaneously at the organization, population, and community levels of analysis. Strategy-making cast in terms of intraorganizational variation, selection, retention, and competition adds an additional level of analysis, which can be studied in its own right, as well as in relation to the other levels. Purposeful variations at the intraorganizational level, for instance, may sometimes look like emergent variations at the organization level, and intraorganizational selection processes can lead to organization-level adaptation (or maladaptation).

2.1.1 Strategy-Making and Organizational Learning

Adopting an evolutionary perspective implies that outcomes are viewed as indeterminate and can only be explained after the fact. This seems almost the exact antipode of the traditional view of strategy, which is to determine in advance the strategic actions that will achieve desired outcomes. There is no conflict, however, when strategy-making is viewed as an organizational learning process. Strategy becomes real when consequential action is taken, often by multiple strategic actors simultaneously. Consequential action commits the company to a course of action that is difficult to reverse (cf. Ghemawat, 1991). That said, thorough preparatory work on deciding such a course of action is of course important. At least equally important, however, is the work that comes after a course of action has been decided on. In highly dynamic environments, the unpredictable interaction and correlation of forces make most strategic plans unreliable by the time they are implemented. Effective strategists in such environments must be able to quickly understand why their plan-based actions produce particular, often unanticipated outcomes. Such strategic recognition provides a basis for taking further strategic actions. Sometimes this involves abandoning the course of action – for instance, exiting from a failing business.

The capacity to consistently align action with stated strategy is the hard-won gain of an organizational learning process. Top management learns what the company's distinctive competencies are, in which product-market domain(s) it can win, what core values provide safe guidance when faced with ambiguous choices, and which objectives are meaningful and worth reaching for. The part of the strategy-making process through which strategic action is deliberately driven in a fairly foreseeable pattern toward desired outcomes is called the *induced* strategy process. But strategy-making also manifests itself as a learning process through the *autonomous* strategy process driven by lower-level managers and employees. Strategic action at higher levels in the management hierarchy benefits from the interpretation of the outcomes of strategic action at lower levels. Progress in this social learning process depends on multilevel interplay between action and cognition. The effectiveness of the sequence of interplay depends on correctly interpreting the results of strategic action at each level, which makes it possible to articulate strategic content for that level. That strategic content then becomes a stepping stone for more encompassing strategic action at the next managerial level, and so on. The autonomous part of the strategy-making process integrates lower-level strategic action to achieve company-level strategic rationality (see Burgelman, 1988). Vectoring the outcomes of the autonomous strategy process by top management provides a basis for amending the corporate strategy (see Section 3.4).

2.1.2 Organizational Ecology and Strategy-Making

Organizational ecology emerged as a new theoretical approach in the mid-1970s (Hannan & Freeman, 1977). The key argument of the theory as originally formulated was roughly as follows. Organizational change must be understood at the level of entire populations of similar organizations, and as the result of replacement and selection rather than of adaptation. For instance, suppose one measured the average characteristics of companies in a particular population – the semiconductor industry, say – in 1960, and did so again in 2000. And suppose one found significant differences in average company characteristics. Organizational ecology posits that these differences do not come about because the incumbent companies have changed, but because of an ongoing process of selection (incumbent companies exiting, usually because of failure) and replacement (new companies with different characteristics entering). Incumbent companies fail in the face of environmental change because organizational inertia prevents them from adapting. In short, organizational inertia causes companies to be selected out of the ecosystem. The rates of founding and disbanding drive strategic change.

During the 1980s, the organizational ecology argument was subtly modified (Hannan & Freeman, 1984), in part because the original formulation begged the question of why companies would be inert in the first place. The major reason for inertia proposed in the revised formulation of the theory is that companies develop routines and procedures to make their behavior reliable, predictable, and accountable to key constituencies such as customers, suppliers, employees, financial analysts, and so on. These attributes allow companies to overcome liabilities of newness, gain legitimacy, and be selected by the environment over others that are less reliable, predictable, and accountable. Companies' very efforts to be reliable, predictable, and accountable, however, make it difficult for them to change in major ways. Hence, the new argument was that environmental selection leads to organizational inertia. There is strong empirical evidence in support of organizational ecology (for a review see Singh & Lumsden, 1990); however, it continues to pose a challenge, because even in the revised theory there is little room for adaptation based on strategy.

The premise of this section (and Element) is that a fruitful integration of organizational ecology and strategy is possible (see Burgelman, 1990 for an earlier effort). The argument, briefly, runs as follows. Almost all companies start small and are subject to liabilities of newness in that they are unknown, are untested, lack legitimacy, and so on (Freeman et al., 1983; Singh et al., 1986; Stinchcombe, 1965). The major force faced by small, new companies is environmental selection. Most young firms do not survive external selection pressures. Organizational ecology provides a useful theoretical framework within which the evolutionary dynamics of these nascent firms can be more clearly understood. Some companies, however, do survive and become large and established. Despite their size, established companies are still subject to the selection force of the external environment, and many succumb to it in the long run. However, these companies have gained the opportunity to substitute internal selection for external selection. Each established company constitutes a unique ecology in itself, and its survival and success depend on how well it takes advantage of its internal ecological processes. Strategy-making is an important part of these processes, which, like the processes at the level of organizational populations, are critically based on the ability to enter new businesses and exit failing ones over time (see Burgelman, 1991 for an earlier discussion; and see Galunic & Weeks, 2017 for a review of intraorganizational ecology).

Intraorganizational variation comes about as the result of individuals (or small groups) seeking to express their special skills and values, and advance their careers, through the pursuit of strategic initiatives. These initiatives draw on existing and/or new competencies and routines, and take the form of new organizational units (e.g., functional, product-based, business-model-based, geographical) within the organization. Selection works through administrative and cultural mechanisms regulating the allocation of resources and attention to different strategic initiatives and associated competencies, routines, and organizational units. Selection operates on competencies and routines as well as on the organizational units containing them. Retention concerns the initiatives that survive in the external environment and grow to be important within the company. It takes the form of organization-level learning about the factors that account for the success of such initiatives. Internal competition arises from different strategic initiatives struggling to obtain the resources they need to grow and increase in importance in the company. Internal competition between strategic initiatives for resource allocation can be tightly linked to the external competition that these initiatives encounter.

2.2 Three Conceptual Tools of Strategy-Making

In the realm of theory, the processes of variation, selection, and retention are general, abstract, and nonexperiential. In the realm of practice, on the other hand, common language describing strategy-making is particular, concrete, and experiential. Business leaders do not use the terminology of pure theory to think and talk about strategy-making, and find it difficult to relate to its formal mathematical and statistical models. Scholars, on the other hand, find it difficult to gain deeper insight when limited to everyday language, and like to do more than produce a coherent and complete narrative of best practice. Conceptual frameworks help bridge the gap between pure theory and best practice (see Winter, 1987). They are specific, substantive, and suggestive. The boxes-and-arrows charts used to represent them can be more readily understood and related to by business leaders and scholars alike, and we use these throughout the Element in the various tools and frameworks we present.

Three tools form the backbone of identifying and analyzing the role of strategy-making in firm evolution at three interrelated levels of analysis: (1) Tool I (also called the strategy diamond): company–environment interface level; (2) Tool II: company level; and (3) Tool III: intracompany level. The evolutionary research lens has strong "zooming" capabilities: from environment and company interface-level forces and their interactions to company-level induced and autonomous strategy processes and their evolving balance, and then to the intracompany-level details of strategic leadership activities involved in these processes. Figure 2 presents these tools.

2.2.1 Tool I: Dynamic Forces Driving Firm Evolution ("Strategy Diamond")

The framework of dynamic forces driving organizational evolution – Tool I in Figure 2, also referred to as the strategy diamond, and Figure 3 – serves to analyze industry-level and company-level processes of variation, selection, and retention and their interplay throughout organizational evolution (see Burgelman, 1994).[5] This framework synthesizes the strategic positioning (Porter, 1980), resource-based view, and dynamic capabilities perspectives (Barney, 1991; Teece, 2007)

---

[5] The "basis of competitive advantage in the industry" of Tool I relates directly to Michael Porter's (1980) framework of industry forces. Tool I thus provides a way to link internal and external strategic forces. Other external forces include technology, complementors, and nonmarket forces such as government regulation.

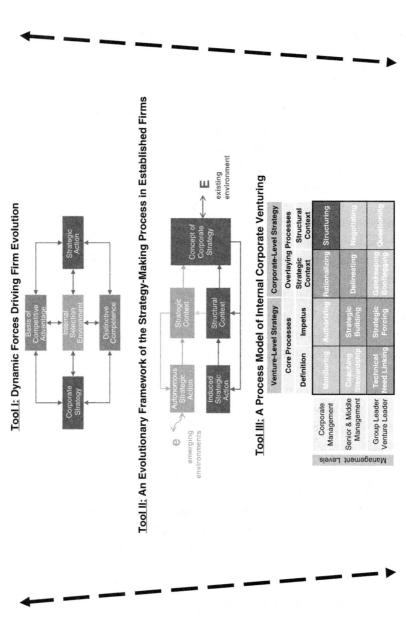

Figure 2 Three interrelated conceptual tools of an evolutionary research lens

Source: Burgelman (2002b: 9).

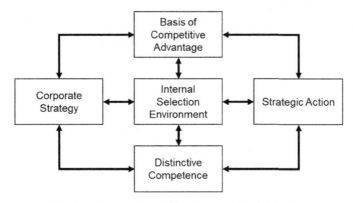

Figure 3 Dynamic forces driving firm evolution
Source: Burgelman (1994).

in strategic management, and the formulation and execution aspects of the strategy-making process (Mintzberg & Waters, 1985).

Tool I comprises five dynamic forces that drive organizational evolution. The *basis of competitive advantage* in the industries in which the company chooses strategic product-market positions is determined by the interplay of external forces that constitute the firm's business ecosystem. *Distinctive competence* encompasses the firm's differentiated skills, resources, and capabilities. *Corporate strategy* reflects CEO and top management beliefs about how the firm should position itself in its business ecosystem and use its distinctive competences to occupy, defend, and leverage these strategic positions. *Strategic action* concerns the firm's consequential actions (whether taken or not taken). The *internal selection environment* mediates – mostly through resource allocation to different business models and product offerings – the links between corporate strategy and strategic action, as well as the coevolution of industry-level sources of competitive advantage and firm-level sources of distinctive competence. These five forces can be aligned or misaligned.

Strategic inflection points. When the normative, technological, economic, and cognitive rules (among others) that determine the basis of competitive advantage in the industry and/or broader ecosystem change (Burgelman & Grove, 2007), the internal selection environment may become misaligned with the external selection environment, and the company risks being selected out and replaced by new competitors. For instance, ecosystem interdependencies can influence a company's ability to respond to new technologies (Kapoor & Lee, 2013) or react to latent disruptive threats from complementors (Adner & Lieberman, 2021). In such situations, the company faces a strategic inflection point (SIP). Confronted with a SIP, the company is entering (or has already entered) a period

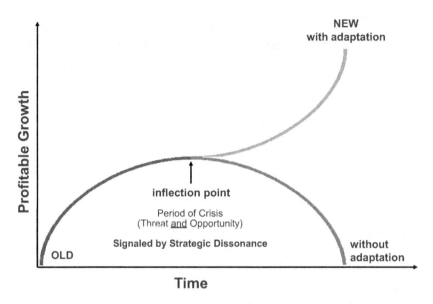

Figure 4 Strategic inflection points and changing the rules of the game
Source: Adapted from Burgelman and Grove (1996: 11).

of crisis during which, if it does not change its strategy, it faces a material threat to its profitable growth prospects and potentially even its demise as an independent entity. If it can change its strategy in time, however, it may be able to get onto a new profitable growth trajectory. Figure 4 illustrates the concept of SIPs.

As suggested in Figure 4, the emergence of a SIP is indicated by growing misalignment between the basis of competitive advantage and the company's distinctive competence, and between the corporate strategy and strategic action within the "strategy diamond." This is typically related to the "strategic disson-ance" among the organization's managers (Burgelman & Grove, 1996). One option available to the company is strategic exit or abandoning a given business and moving to a different growth trajectory or even a new ecosystem, where alignment becomes important once again. For instance, this is what Intel eventually did (Burgelman, 1994), exiting the DRAM industry and committing to the microprocessor industry (Section 3.2). Another option is the corporate split, which is particularly useful under conditions of ecosystem bifurcation, as evidenced by the split of HP in 2015 by its CEO Meg Whitman (Section 4.2).

2.2.2 Tool II: Evolutionary Framework of the Strategy-Making Process

Zooming in on the strategy-making process, the framework of induced and autonomous strategy processes – Tool II in Figures 2 and 5 – further illuminates the role of internal variation, selection, and retention.

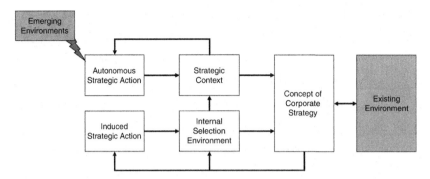

Figure 5 Evolutionary framework of the strategy-making process
Source: Burgelman (2002a).

Autonomous strategic action refers to action taken without top-down direction from management by organizational members that can result in new initiatives, such as the emergence of microprocessors at Intel or printers at HP. Autonomous strategic action is typically the source of internal variation in strategic initiatives and varied experiments.

Induced strategic action refers to action taken by organizational members following top management direction – for instance, pursuing specific R&D projects (such as incremental product innovation) aligned with the structural organizational context. Both induced and autonomous strategic actions can result in new initiatives that are selected and retained (or not) through the organizational structural and strategic context. The good functioning of the internal selection environment (i.e., producing sufficient variety of new initiatives) is important to ensure organizational renewal, particularly when the external environment might be evolving.

We also propose that as an autonomous initiative gains impetus in the strategy-making process, a critical top management role is to evaluate first, the extent to which the autonomous opportunity has been validated (through the process of strategic context determination), and second, the extent to which available cash reserves are sufficient to protect the company from disaster in case the scaled-up autonomous initiative ultimately fails (see Table 2). This suggests four possible strategic choices: (1) "safe bet": validated opportunity and sufficient cash reserves; (2) "bet the company": validated opportunity but insufficient reserves; (3) "wait to bet": not-yet-validated opportunity and sufficient cash reserves, which also raises the question *how long* to wait; and (4) "desperate bet": not-yet-validated opportunity and insufficient cash reserves. Having to "bet the company" and "desperate bet" are the strategic choices to avoid.

Table 2 Critical role of top management related to autonomous strategic opportunities

		Autonomous opportunity	
		Validated	*Not yet validated*
Cash reserves	*Sufficient*[a]	Safe bet	Wait to bet: but how long?
	Insufficient	Bet the company	Desperate bet

[a] To protect the company from disaster in case scaled-up autonomous initiative fails.
Source: Burgelman and Grove (2007).

Over time, the outcomes of the combined internal and external selection processes operating on induced and autonomous variations can either ensure renewal or lead to organizational demise. Like the role of founding and disbanding as sources of population-level change in organizational ecology, entry into new businesses and exit from existing ones are sources of corporate-level transformation in the internal ecology of strategy-making (Burgelman, 1991).

2.2.3 Tool III: Process Model of Strategy-Making (Internal Corporate Venturing)

The process model – Tool III in Figures 2 and 6 – helps zoom in further on the patterns of detailed strategic leadership activities involved in the internal variation, selection, retention, and competition processes associated with entering into new businesses.

This tool highlights the simultaneous strategic actions of multiple actors distributed throughout the organization that together contribute to strategy-making. The research of Burgelman at Intel, for instance, showed that coordinating the simultaneous actions of multiple strategic actors into a coherent pattern of strategy-making, especially in the face of environmental change, was a major challenge. During the tenure of Gordon Moore as CEO, coordination was achieved primarily through the internal selection environment. During Andy Grove's tenure as CEO, Intel achieved coordination through strategic direction set by top management.

Coordination through internal selection is a powerful manifestation of self-organization, which depends on "mutually dependent criteria of action (utility functions)" (Prigogine, 1980). Such criteria seem closely related to the idea of "focal points," which is used by some scholars to give operational meaning to culture (cf. Schelling, 1963).[6] Andy Grove strongly focused Intel's induced

---

[6] According to Schelling, focal points facilitate coordination without communication. More generally, they are ideas, values, criteria, and the like around which the organization's members

Key Activities		Core Processes		Overlaying Processes	
		Definition	Impetus	Strategic Context	Structural Context
Management Levels	Corporate Management	Monitoring	Authorizing	Rationalizing	Structuring
			Organizational Championing	Selecting	
	Senior & Middle Management	Coaching Stewardship	Strategic Building	Delineating	Negotiating
			Product Championing		
	Group Leader Venture Leader	Technical and Lead Linking	Strategic Forcing	Gatekeeping Idea Generating Bootlegging	Questioning

Figure 6 Process model of strategy-making (internal corporate venturing)
Source: Burgelman (1983c).

strategy process on the core microprocessor business and concentrated strategic decision-making at the top, thereby limiting the role of lower levels mostly to the execution of the official corporate strategy. While tightly coordinated and extremely successful in executing the core business strategy, Intel's strategy-making process also became severely constraining. The core business strategy and associated structural context at Intel had an overwhelming influence on the definition of new business opportunities. The ICV process-model tool and several derivatives are discussed in further detail in Section 3.

Taking a broader view, there are clear links between process modeling and ecological notions of self-organization (Thiétart & Forgues, 1995). Ilya Prigogine (1980), Nobel laureate in Chemistry, uses the Lotka–Volterra equations of prey–predator competition, which are part of the conceptual foundation of organizational ecology, in a discussion of self-organization to examine "structural stability." According to Prigogine (1980: 109), structural stability "seems to express in the most compact way the idea of innovation, the appearance of a new mechanism and a new species, which were initially absent in the system." He views "structure" as resulting from the actions (choices) of multiple actors, having "in part at least mutually dependent criteria of action (utility functions)" (p. 126). Referring to the "baroque of the natural world," he posits:

> ecosystems contain many more species than would be "necessary" if biological efficiency alone were an organizing principle. This "over creativity" of nature emerges naturally from the type of description being suggested here,

---

naturally coalesce or toward which they naturally converge. Focal points are useful for operationalizing corporate culture as a rational concept.

in which "mutations" and "innovations" occur stochastically and are integrated into the system by the deterministic relations prevailing at the moment.
Thus, we have in this perspective the constant generation of "new types" and
"new ideas" that may be incorporated into the structure of the system, causing
its continual evolution (p. 128).

Keeping in mind the pitfalls of the fallacy of unwarranted analogy (cf. Merton,
1957), there seems nevertheless to be a potentially interesting isomorphism
between Prigogine's analysis and the analysis of the role of the *induced* and
autonomous processes in strategy-making. *Autonomous* initiatives generate
innovations (new ideas) in the organization, but they are viable only if they
can be integrated into the corporate strategy and eventually become part of the
induced strategy process. Strategic context determination is the part of the
process through which this integration is attempted. How strategic context
determination works, and what determines its success, may be the central
issue in a theory of corporate entrepreneurship (Burgelman, 1983a).

2.3 The Crucial Role of the Internal Selection Environment

The insights generated with the three tools of the evolutionary lens for studying
strategy-making processes indicate the importance of the internal selection
environment for maintaining organizational adaptation and longevity. They
also shed light on several important dilemmas occurring during the dynamics
of organizational adaptation that raise further questions: How much of
a company's resources should be devoted, over time, to the induced and
autonomous strategy processes, respectively? How to manage the difficulties
of balancing opposing orientations (toward variation or selection) within the
strategy-making process? These questions have potentially important theoretical and normative implications for designing the internal ecology of strategy-
making as an adaptive organizational capability.

2.3.1 Creating a Change-Ready Internal Selection Environment

These insights suggest that the organization's internal selection environment
needs to be change-ready. We argue that such readiness has four critical aspects.
First, resource allocation needs to reflect competitive reality of the evolving
business ecosystem, as resource allocation shapes the distinctive capabilities of
the organization (Burgelman, 1994; Maritan & Lee, 2017), influences firm
boundaries (Levinthal, 2017), and drives innovation (Gerstner et al., 2013;
Kaplan, 2008; Klingebiel & Rammer, 2014). However, importantly, this
depends on clearly identifying the current winners and losers in the competitive
environment. Second, strategic planning requires forums for debating new

opportunities. This means there must be conversations between those who are making money today (in search of fit) and those who promise to make money tomorrow (in search of evolvability), but with today (rationally) prevailing over tomorrow most of the time. Third, top and senior managers need to be capable of strategic recognition, as this helps identify tomorrow's viable new opportunities and to secure resources for their pursuit. Finally, there needs to be strategic leadership that is capable and willing to move from strategic recognition to strategic action, which depends on insight and courage (because it involves difficult-to-reverse commitments).

2.3.2 The Internal Selection Environment Shapes the Strategy-Making Process

We also argue that strategy-making as an adaptive organizational capability depends on the combination of induced and autonomous strategy processes throughout a company's evolution. This does not imply that the weighting of these two processes should be constant over time. During any given period, and given a specific resource level, top management explicitly or implicitly makes tradeoffs in resources allocated to induced and autonomous strategic initiatives. In principle, the changing weights should reflect the key strategic challenges faced by the company during a particular period, and whether the dominant concern is exploiting existing opportunities or developing new ones. But both processes should be always in play in the internal selection environment (Burgelman, 1983b; Prigogine, 1980; Sahal, 1979).

2.3.3 The Effectiveness of the Internal Selection Environment Depends on Simultaneity

Even if we could calculate the optimal proportion of induced and autonomous strategic initiatives at any given time, we would still face the question of whether the behaviors associated with induced (variation-reducing) and autonomous (variation-increasing) strategy processes are fundamentally at odds with each other, or can be effectively pursued simultaneously. Strategic context determination processes appear to be the crucial nexus between exploration and exploitation, and crucial to effectively balancing induced and autonomous strategy processes. They help turn exploration efforts into new exploitation opportunities. Strategic context determination processes complement a company's structural context in important ways. They offer the possibility to suspend the selective effects of the structural context, which almost inevitably tends to become fine-tuned for supporting top management's current strategic intent. They also serve to create linkages between autonomous strategic action and the company's strategy, thereby amending it. The capacity to activate and successfully complete such processes depends critically on the cognitive, political, and general management abilities of middle-level executives (discussed further in Section 3). A company's ability to activate and complete strategic context determination and dissolution processes can be usefully viewed as a measure of the intelligence of its internal selection environment.

2.3.4 Internal Selection Environment Effectiveness and CEO Strategic Leadership

The internal selection environment can be strongly influenced by the approach of the CEO and top management team. Research into HP's evolution (discussed further in Section 4) has shown that an organization's long-term adaptation, spanning multiple generations of CEOs, critically depends on maintaining the strategic renewal capability of its internal ecology of strategy-making. This conceptual separation between the internal selection environment as emergent property and the influence of any given top management team during a company's history provides a foundation for novel directions in further research about the role of strategy-making in firm evolution and how managers can collectively and successively contribute to this process.

2.4 Conclusion

The intraorganizational ecological perspective on strategy-making proposes the need to balance the variation-reducing (induced) and variation-increasing (autonomous) processes in the organization's internal selection environment. One process leads to relative inertia and incremental adjustments, while the other expands the organization's domain and renews its distinctive competence base, countering inertia and serving adaptation through strategic renewal. The balancing of these processes constitutes the fourth level in the hierarchy of an ecological system, which comprises organization, population, and community levels. The effectiveness of the internal selection environment may be at the heart of strategy-making as an adaptive organizational capability.

The intraorganizational ecology perspective also extends Mintzberg's (1978) strategy-making framework by documenting some of the sources of emergent strategy more explicitly, by further elucidating the organizational decision processes through which emergent strategies become part of realized strategies (Mirabeau & Maguire, 2014), and by identifying simultaneous and sequential feedback mechanisms between realized and intended strategy.

3 Process Models of Strategy-Making in Organizational Evolution

One of the more enduring process models of organizational evolution is the B–B process model. Building on Bower's (1970) study of strategic capital investment projects, this model connects the project and corporate levels of analysis to depict simultaneous as well as sequential strategic activities. It is a useful conceptual tool (Tool III in Section 2) for depicting the pattern of activities of managers involved in intraorganizational ecological processes. The B–B process model augments the tool kit of a theoretical perspective that shifts the locus of selection from the firm as a whole to classes of strategic action within it, and views managing intraorganizational ecological processes as a means by which the firm can achieve the learning benefits of both external and internal selection (Barnett et al., 1994; Burgelman, 1991, 1994; Rumelt et al., 1994). The B–B model is useful in examining the pattern of activities by managerial actors that produce higher-level outcomes. For instance, it helps untangle the pattern of activities exercised by managers positioned at the top, middle, and operational levels of the organizational hierarchy that contributes to the strategic exit from underperforming businesses at the organization level (Burgelman, 1996).

The B–B process model comprises both business- and corporate-level strategy-making and can depict the sequential and simultaneous activities of different strata of management in each of these levels. To do so, it features interlocking key activities (processes) that constitute the major driving forces in the strategy-making: *definition, impetus, strategic context determination*, and *structural context determination*. The *structural context* and *strategic context* parts of the process model constitute the internal selection environment within which the business-level parts take shape, and through which the corporate-level strategic issues are brought into focus.

The *definition process* encompasses the technical-economic managerial activities that initiate strategy-making. As the definition process unfolds, the nascent strategic idea evolves into a concrete new product, process, or system around which an early team forms. As a result of successful proof points (often technical and market development efforts), the idea can begin to take shape within the business organization. The *impetus process* comprises the managerial activities to gain and maintain support in the organization. Major impetus occurs when strategic change moves from a lower level in the organization to a higher one, because it is normally around this time that it acquires its own structure, general manager, and operating budget, thus becoming an embryonic new business operation within the organization. The impetus process reaches its conclusion in the decision to integrate this new strategy into the operating system of the corporation.

To cross this threshold, the new strategy must become integrated into the corporation's existing concept of strategy. This involves complex interactions between managers in the process of *strategic context determination*: the political process through which middle-level managers attempt to convince top management that the current concept of strategy needs to be changed. The *structural context* part of the process model maps the selective forces associated with the rules governing resource allocation and strategic debate, and the managerial activities involved in attempts to change the rules. As such, *structural context* refers to the various organizational and administrative mechanisms put in place by corporate management to implement the current corporate strategy. It operates as a selection mechanism on the strategic behavior of operational and middle-level managers.

The B–B process model is based on qualitative pattern-matching and does not aim to cover the entire range of issues associated with strategic change. While this pattern-matching is normally done carefully and objectively, the patterns found necessarily reflect the conceptual lens used. Consequently, process models show the pattern of managerial activities through which a strategic outcome such as ICV or strategic business exit (SBE) comes about, and explain variation in this pattern. Process models of strategy-making using the B–B approach help illuminate the working of internal selection processes. Documenting the multilevel interplays of managerial activities involved in strategic context determination and dissolution elucidates the subtle intertwining of internal selection and coordination, and the value-added activities of middle-level managers. Documenting the intrafirm Schumpeterian innovation process also informs the resource-based view of the firm, which examines how firm-specific resource combinations become sources of competitive advantage. Below, we summarize four such models: the original model of ICV (Section 3.1), the model of SBE (Section 3.2), the model of corporate venture capital (CVC; Section 3.3), and the ecosystem-level model of disruption beyond the firm (Section 3.4).

3.1 Within the Firm: The Internal Corporate Venturing Process Model

This model (for the original study see Burgelman, 1983c) investigates the processes through which a diversified major firm transforms R&D activities at the frontier of corporate technology into new businesses through ICV. The research was carried out in one large, USA-based, diversified high-technology firm. The case firm had traditionally produced and sold various commodities in high volumes, but had also tried to diversify through the internal development of new products, processes, and systems. In doing so, it hoped to get closer to the final user or consumer and capture a greater portion of the total value added in the chain from raw materials to end products. A longitudinal processual approach (Pettigrew, 1990) was adopted, where the ICV process was studied exhaustively in one setting. Data were collected on six ongoing ICV projects that were in various stages of development. The historical development of each case was traced and the progress of each case during a fifteen-month research period was observed and recorded. These materials formed the basis for a comparative analysis of the six projects.

Figure 7 maps the activities involved in ICV onto the B–B process model. It shows how the strategic process in and around ICV is constituted by a set of key activities (the shaded area) and by a set of more peripheral activities (the nonshaded area). These activities are situated at the corporate, middle, and operational levels of management. Figure 8, which can be superimposed on Figure 7, shows how these different activities interlock with each other, forming a pattern of connections. The relative importance of activities is indicated by the different types of line segments. The data also suggested a sequential flow of activities in this pattern, as indicated by the numbers in Figure 8.

This process model shows that ICV is primarily a bottom-up (*autonomous*) process and depicts the key role performed by middle management. Entrepreneurial activities at the operational and middle levels (1, 2, 3) interact with the selective mechanisms of the structural context (5). These selective mechanisms can be circumvented by activating, through organizational

Key Activities		Core Processes		Overlaying Processes	
		Definition	Impetus	Strategic Context	Structural Context
Management Levels	Corporate Management	Monitoring	Authorizing	Rationalizing	Structuring
			Organizational Championing	*Selecting*	
	Senior & Middle Management	Coaching Stewardship	Strategic Building	Delineating	Negotiating
			Product Championing		
	Group Leader Venture Leader	Technical and Lead Linking	Strategic Forcing	Gatekeeping Idea Generating Bootlegging	Questioning

Figure 7 Key and peripheral activities in a process model of ICV
Source: Burgelman (1983c: 230).

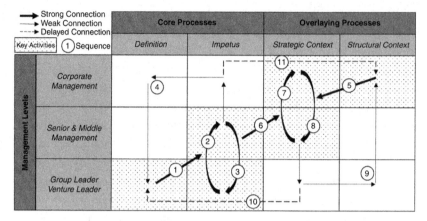

Figure 8 Flow of activities in a process model of ICV
Source: Burgelman (1983c: 230).

championing (6), the strategic context, which allows successful ICV projects to become retroactively rationalized by corporate management in fields of new business delineated by the middle level (7, 8). These parts of the pattern, represented by the solid line segments in Figure 8, constitute the major forces generated and encountered by ICV projects.

The finely dotted lines in Figure 8 (4, 9) represent the connections between the more peripheral activities in the ICV process and their linkages with the key activities. Corporate management monitor resource allocation to ICV projects. Middle-level managers manage these resources and facilitate collaboration between R&D and businesspeople in the definition of new business opportunities; however, these activities support the definition process rather than driving it. In the same fashion, authorizing further development is clearly the prerogative of corporate management, but this is a result, not a determinant, of the impetus process. In the strategic context determination process, gatekeeping, idea-generating, and bootlegging activities by operational-level participants were all found to be important in developing a basis for further definition processes, but are a result of the process rather than a determinant. In the process of structural context determination, questioning of the structural context by operational-level participants and efforts by middle managers to negotiate changes in it are reactive rather than primary.

The broken line segments in Figure 8 (10, 11) indicate two important delayed effects in the ICV process. First, the successful activation of the process of strategic context determination encourages further entrepreneurial activities at the operational level, thus creating a feedforward loop to the definition process (10). Second, corporate management attempts to influence the ICV process, primarily through its manipulations of the structural context. These manipulations appear to be in reaction to the results of previously authorized ICV projects. This creates a feedback loop (11) between the core and overlaying processes.

One important finding of this study is that the motor of corporate entrepreneurship (or even strategic innovation more broadly) resides in the autonomous strategic initiatives of individuals at the operational levels in the organization. However, because of their very nature, autonomous initiatives are likely to encounter serious difficulties in the diversified major firm. Their proponents must often cope with problems of resource allocation because they attempt to achieve objectives that are beyond the corporation's horizons. Because such initiatives require unusual, even unorthodox, approaches, they create managerial dilemmas that are temporarily resolved through the deliberate neglect of administrative issues during the early stages.

This study also elucidates the key role of middle-level managers in the strategy-making process. The middle manager performs the crucial role of linking successful autonomous strategic behavior at the operational level with the corporate concept of strategy. Both the continuation of the impetus process and the change of the corporate strategy through the activation of the process of strategic context determination depend on the conceptual and political capabilities of managers at this level. Relatedly, corporate management's role seems to be limited to the retroactive rationalization of autonomous strategic initiatives that have been selected by both the external environment and the internal environment. When they do intervene, top management's direct influence is through the manipulation of structural context.

This study can also be related to the validity of rational versus natural selection models to explain organizational growth and development (Aldrich, 1979; Pfeffer & Salancik, 1978; Weick, 1979). The multilayered picture of the strategic management process presented here suggests that these strategic choice processes, when exercised during innovation initiatives, take the form of experimentation and selection, in line with organizational evolutionary theory rather than the strategic planning or rational actor approach. Relatedly, this study also illustrates that large, complex business organizations have separate variation and selection mechanisms. Previously unplanned, radically new projects at the product-market level are generated from the relatively unique combination of productive resources of such firms. Not all of these projects are retained – not so much because the market may turn out to be unreceptive, but because they must overcome the selection mechanisms in the internal selection environment of the firm, which reflect, normally, the current strategy of the corporation, that is, the retained wisdom of previously selected strategic behavior. Thus, the experimentation and selection model draws attention to the possibility that firms may adopt externally unviable projects, or fail to adopt externally viable ones, and provides a clue as to why firms occasionally produce strange innovations.

The insights generated by the present study also have some implications for further research on the management of the strategy-making process in general. Comparative research studies of a longitudinal-processual nature, carried out at multiple levels of analysis, are necessary to document and conceptualize the multilayered, loosely coupled network of interlocking, simultaneous, and sequential key activities that constitute the strategy-making process. Following Bower (1970), the study found it useful to focus the research on particular strategic projects rather than on the strategy-making process in general. This is consistent with Quinn's (1980: 52) observation that top managers "deal with the logic of each subsystem of strategy formulation largely on its own merits and usually with a different subset of people." A concrete focus, it would seem, is more likely to produce data on the vicious circles, dilemmas, paradoxes, and creative tensions that are embedded in the strategy-making process.

3.2 Within the Firm: Strategic Business Exit Process Model

This model (see Burgelman, 1996 for the original study) is based on the Intel Corporation's SBE in the mid-1980s from the dynamic random access memory (DRAM) business, which had been its core business during the 1970s. The data on Intel's exit from DRAMs were part of a longitudinal field study of the evolution of its corporate strategy. The study was based on a longitudinal, two-stage, nested case study design within one corporate setting (e.g., Leonard-Barton, 1990; Yin, 2018). While concentrating on one organization with more than twenty years of continuity in leadership limits the generalizability of the findings, it also made it possible to gain access to sources with intimate knowledge of the details of the firm's evolution.

The construction of the SBE process model involved an iterative approach of qualitative pattern-matching, moving back and forth between the B–B process model and the DRAM exit data. Qualitative pattern-matching suggested that the overall structure of the ICV process model was useful to conceptualize the strategy-making involved in SBE. Qualitative pattern-matching also revealed, however, that the managerial activities involved in SBE, and the linkages between them, were quite different. This effort yielded new categories to conceptualize the managerial activities involved in SBE. These are shown in Figure 9.

	Levels of Strategy Making			
Driving Activities	Business Level		Corporate Level	
	Definition	Impetus	Strategic Context	Structural Context
Top Management	Equivocating	Authorizing	Strategic Recognition and Rationalizing	Structuring
			Selecting	
Middle Management (Functional)	Inertial Competence Deployment	Undermining Resource Shifting	Technological Uncoupling	Negotiating Structural Change
	Falling Behind			
Operational Management (Business)	Unlinking	Repositioning	Questioning Strategy	Questioning Structure

Figure 9 Managerial activities in a process model of SBE
Source: Burgelman (1996: 197).

Figure 9 shows that each part of the SBE process model involved top, middle, and operations-level managerial activities. The relations between the operational and middle levels are viewed in terms of responsibilities rather than hierarchy. Intel was a multibusiness firm, but its organizational structure maintained a strong functional dimension, with managers of the different product divisions needing to obtain R&D and manufacturing support for their products from the functional units. This is reflected in Figure 9: operational managers were business managers who interacted with the product-market environment and were primarily concerned with business strategy-level issues, while middle managers were functional managers primarily concerned with maintaining and developing the firm's distinctive technological competencies and with resource-allocation issues. Top managers, on the other hand, were primarily concerned with corporate strategy-level issues. Some activities – shown in bold type – drove the SBE process more strongly than others.

Figure 10, which can be superimposed on Figure 9, shows how these different activities interlock with each other, forming a pattern of connections. The arrows indicate the dominant direction of influence among the key managerial activities. The relative importance of activities is indicated by the different types of line segments. The rough sequential and simultaneous flow of the activities in this pattern is indicated by the numbers.

The solid lines in Figure 10 identify the activities that were strongest in driving the SBE process. Inertial competence deployment of middle-level managers (1) led to the unlinking of market needs and Intel DRAM products. Operational and middle-level managerial activities at the business level (3, 4)

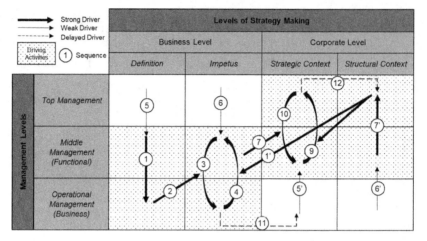

Figure 10 Flow of activities in a process model of SBE
Source: Burgelman (1996: 198).

responded to the selective pressures of the structural context (1') favoring other businesses, and to DRAMs falling behind (2) in the market. At the corporate level, the undermining of the DRAM business (7) resulting from resource shifts, combined with the continued selective pressures from the structural context (8), set the stage for middle managers' technological uncoupling activities and top management's strategic recognition and rationalization of the exit from DRAMs (9, 10). The undermining of the DRAM business was unsuccessfully countered by the efforts of some DRAM middle-level managers to negotiate changes in Intel's structural context (7').

The finely dotted lines in Figure 10 represent the set of activities that were weak drivers of the SBE process. At the business strategy level, top management's equivocation about the importance of DRAMs for Intel (5) led them to continue to invest heavily in DRAM R&D, which reinforced the inertial competence deployment of middle-level managers (definition). On the other hand, top management authorized (6) incremental shifting of scarce manufacturing resources from DRAMs to other businesses (impetus). At the corporate strategy level, operational managers associated with the DRAM business questioned Intel's business strategy in DRAMs (5') (strategic context). Operational-level managers also questioned some aspects of the structural context, in particular the resource allocation rule, as shifts in resource allocation were made and authorized (6').

The broken line segments in Figure 10 indicate two delayed effects in the SBE process. First, a last-ditch, unsuccessful effort was launched by a DRAM business manager to change the strategic context of the DRAM business in 1985 (11).

Second, the decision to exit from DRAMs led top management to reconsider some aspects of Intel's structural context (12).

This study shows how process models of substantive areas of strategy-making such as SBE provide windows into the "black box" of strategy-making in complex organizations. The approach is positive descriptive, and it helps to identify and explain paradoxes, vicious circles, dilemmas, and tensions in the strategy-making process that derive from the activities of managers who are differentially situated in the organization and respond to different external and internal pressures. For instance, the process model of SBE shows how the process technology competence that allowed Intel to be the first successful mover in DRAMs paradoxically also bore the seeds of its later failure in DRAMs. It also explains how a vicious circle ("death spiral") in resource allocation to DRAMs resulted from some middle-level managers' inertial deployment of process technology competence, which failed to meet competitive challenges in DRAMs, while others responded to the internal pressures of the structural context by moving scarce manufacturing capacity away from DRAMs.

This study also shows how developing a grounded process model for a substantive area such as SBE helps produce categories and concepts that, while somewhat rudimentary and evocative, are closely tied to the phenomenon and enrich the repertoire for conceptualization. In this respect, the study identified unlinking and repositioning; resource shifting and technological uncoupling; and strategic recognition and structuring as key categories of managerial activity, performed by different levels of management, that shaped the SBE process. The study also showed how these activities brought about the dissolution of the strategic context of a core business of the firm. Linked together in the process model, these categories and concepts depict the complex pattern of managerial activities and organizational forces associated with the SBE phenomenon in a parsimonious way and show the underlying order and sources of rationality in a process that, on the surface, looks chaotic.

Relatedly, a comparison of the process model of SBE to process models of other substantive areas of strategy-making provides additional insight. The SBE process differed in several respects from the process of ICV (Burgelman, 1983c). New business development through ICV was structurally separated from mainstream operations using a new venture division. This purposefully protected new businesses from internal competition for resources for a while, and provided some leeway for operational-level product championing and middle-level organizational championing activities. Strategic context determination for a new venture was expected to involve a positive, upward spiral of growth. SBE, in contrast, took place in an integrated organizational structure where the DRAM business could not escape internal competition for resources with other businesses. Strategic context dissolution of memory businesses involved negative, downward spirals of decline. This made product championing and organizational championing for memory businesses impossible tasks, like swimming against an overwhelming tide.

The process model of SBE supports theory that views the notion that top management defines a strategy that is then expeditiously implemented as an incomplete representation of strategy-making and enactment processes (e.g., Mintzberg, 1978; Mintzberg & Waters, 1985; Quinn, 1989; Weick, 1979) and of organizational change more broadly defined (Grinyer & McKiernan, 1990; Levinthal, 1991; Pettigrew, 1990). The SBE process model underscores the difficulty of establishing who the relevant "actor" is (Allison & Zelikow, 1999) when considering strategic interaction involving complex organizations, and it provides additional insight into the internal sources of inertia in strategic response and the myopia of organizational learning (Levinthal & March, 1993). The model also helps to show why the application of formal theories of competitive interaction, such as game theory (Camerer, 1991; Saloner, 1991), is problematic when complex organizations are involved.

Another insight from this study is that the process model documents matrixed levels of management by levels of strategy-making, which helps to elucidate the interplays between business- and corporate-level strategy-making. Conceptualizing the complete process, depicting simultaneous as well as sequential managerial activities and contextual forces, also helps to illuminate the difficulties in establishing when exactly the strategic exit decision is made, and when SBE occurs. As a diagnostic tool, it may draw top management's attention to business-level strategic activities that are already paving the way for an exit, but of which the corporate-level strategic implications have not yet been fully realized, and vice versa. It may also help top management to assess more carefully the evolving links between business-level product-market issues and corporate-level competence issues.

This study also reveals that generic strategy may be a more enduring feature of a company than its substantive strategy. Intel's generic strategy based on differentiation and product leadership endured in DRAM for several product generations in the face of the changing basis of competitive advantage in the industry, which favored the cost leadership-based generic strategy of new entrants. After the exit from DRAM, the differentiation-based generic strategy remained in force, having found a new substantive expression in microprocessors (Burgelman et al., 1997).

Finally, by elucidating internal selection processes, process models of strategy-making also contribute to the debate concerning the prevalence of

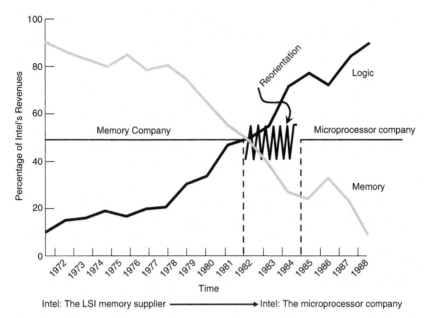

Figure 11 Intel's transformation from memory company to microcomputer company

Source: Burgelman (2002b: 122).

punctuated equilibrium models of strategic change (e.g., Gersick, 1991; Romanelli & Tushman, 1994; Tushman & Romanelli, 1985). Intel's transformation from a memory into a microcomputer company seems at first to have been a rather abrupt organization-level change taking place in the 1984–1985 time frame. A closer look at the strategy-making processes that played out in the late 1970s to mid-1980s time frame, however, reveals that the organization-level change was the culmination of gradual replacement of memory by microprocessors as Intel's core business – a change that took top management a relatively long time to come to grips with. Figure 11 shows this.

The process model thus calls into question the universal applicability of the punctuated equilibrium model, and may help to establish more precisely how and when strategic change takes place. In other words, strategic change may take place, or at least begin, before it is recognized or acknowledged as such by top management due to the activities by the operational and middle-level managers.

3.3 Within the Firm: The Corporate Venture Capital Process Model

As noted in Section 2, in highly dynamic technological environments, companies may face insufficient variation despite having a highly active autonomous strategy process. Adopting CVC as an innovative capability has many features that make it potentially effective for combining internal sources of innovation with external innovation: (1) it helps to keep pace with the innovation happening externally without trying to internalize everything; (2) it helps in exploring far-out bets with lower capital requirements than outright acquisition; and (3) it eases the strain on operational resources by leveraging start-ups' resources to multiply corporate innovation and R&D efforts.

Based on several months of research into JetBlue Technology Ventures (JTV), the CVC arm of JetBlue Airways, including interviews with top executives and public archival material (Burgelman & Sridharan, 2021), we constructed a B–B process model of JTV's strategy-making. The construction of the CVC process model involved an iterative approach of qualitative pattern-matching, moving back and forth between the B–B process model and the JTV CVC data. Qualitative pattern-matching suggested that the overall structure of the B–B process model was useful to conceptualize the strategy-making involved in CVC. It also revealed, however, that the managerial activities involved in CVC, and the linkages between them, were quite different. This effort yielded new categories to conceptualize the managerial activities involved, shown in Figure 12.

Based on our data, the CVC process model shown in Figure 12 reflects that JetBlue's core business strategy was clearly defined and well understood

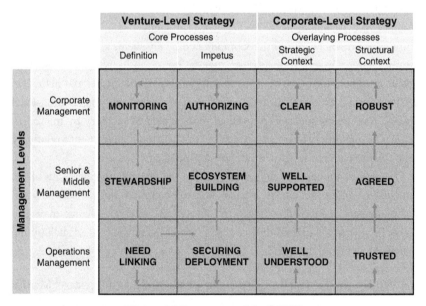

Figure 12 Process model of CVC
Source: Burgelman and Sridharan (2021: 33).

throughout the organization; in other words, the *strategic context* part of the process was relatively fixed, and did not need to be changed to integrate the innovations brought by JTV's start-up innovations. The *structural context* for CVC-corporate relations was also robustly designed. Hence, Figure 12 shows how the overlaying processes provided unequivocal feed-forward corporate management guidance to the core definition and impetus parts of the B–B process model to highlight CVC-driven external innovation activities, and the feedback the core processes provided to reinforce the corporate management guidance. This model shown in Figure 12 applied to the short- and mid-term strategic time horizons of JetBlue: 40 percent of investments focused on near-term benefits (zero to eighteen months) and 50 percent focused on benefits within a medium time horizon (two to five years). Note that an additional application of the B–B process model could have focused on the last 10 percent of the investments, which was focused on innovations that could impact JetBlue in the long term (seven years and beyond). In that case, however, the corporate strategy related to new business opportunities would be less well defined (as it is in ICV), and consequently the strategic context part of the process model would be less tightly determined and would have to allow for CVC initiatives to drive changes to the corporate strategy. This application of the B–B process model was not pursued in the JTV research.

Figure 12 shows that each part of the CVC process model involved top, middle, and operations-level managerial activities. The relations between the operational and middle levels are viewed in terms of responsibilities rather than hierarchy. In the *definition* part of the process, operational managers were JetBlue managers who interacted with the CVC personnel to perform *need linking* of the core business to potential external innovative solutions; middle managers were JetBlue functional managers primarily concerned with *steward-ship* of resource allocation in developing the firm's distinctive technological competencies in collaboration with CVC management; and top managers were primarily concerned with *monitoring* the core business-CVC collaboration from the corporate strategy-level perspective.

In the *impetus* process, top management's main role was *authorizing* the investments made by the CVC; the middle management of the CVC played an important role in *ecosystem building* for the start-ups it invested in and for broadening the potential product-market scope of JetBlue, as it intended to gradually redefine itself as a "travel" company rather than an airline services company; at the same time, JetBlue operational managers collaborated with CVC personnel and the start-up venture personnel in securing deployment activities. As Figure 12 shows, some managerial activities – shown by larger arrows – were stronger in driving the CVC process than others.

This model provides a link with the research on open innovation that prom-
ulgates connections between the firm and its ecosystem (Bogers et al., 2018;
Chesbrough & Appleyard, 2007) and sets the stage for our next model, which
takes us beyond the boundaries of the firm.

3.4 Beyond the Firm: The Business-Model Disruption Process Model

This process model (for the original study, see Snihur et al., 2018) tracks
processes unleashed by a disruptive innovator in its ecosystem, using the B–B
process model to theorize these processes beyond the firm. The underlying
research investigated the early years of Salesforce (1999–2006), during which it
emerged as the leader in on-demand customer relations management software
and instigated the emergence and development of the cloud ecosystem[7] around
the concept of software-as-a-service (SaaS). Through an iterative process of
coding the available historical information, analyzing the existing literature,
and broader conceptual reasoning about temporal and evolutionary dynamics,
the study develops a parsimonious process model of the role of framing and
adaptation in business-model disruption.

In this case, the B–B model was adapted to study ecosystem-level outcomes, in
particular the ecosystem value proposition (Thomas et al., 2022). As structures of
value codiscovery and coproduction, ecosystems feature relationships that are
"not fully hierarchically controlled" (Jacobides et al., 2018: 2264) and which are
instead informal, using mechanisms such as mutual understandings of participant
relationships, role definitions, and technological architecture (Adner, 2017;
Jacobides et al., 2018; Thomas & Ritala, 2022). As such, by disentangling the
pattern of activities carried out by various ecosystem actors, such as the disruptor,
incumbent, customers, partners, and the media, the B–B process model was able
to provide insight into the emergence of the Salesforce cloud ecosystem.

Transposing the B–B process model from the intraorganizational to the
ecosystem context helped elucidate the generative mechanisms of ecosystem
evolution by showing how the activities of ecosystem actors combine to generate strategic outcomes at the level of the ecosystem (rather than the organization). Thus, in contrast to the previous B–B studies, the level of analysis is the
ecosystem, and the unit of analysis is the process (or processes) associated with
business-model disruption. The process model helps examine the interactions,
alignment, and misalignment of distinct ecosystem actors during disruption, its

---

[7] This is where companies take advantage of centrally provided computing resources over the
Internet ("the cloud"), accessing them most often by paying a subscription fee for a service,
instead of owning or renting applications and storage space (see Marston et al., 2011).

key advantage being the depiction of simultaneous as well as sequential activities that might result in nonlinear (e.g., circular or iterative) dynamics. This is particularly important in the case of disruptive innovation, where a time lag between the actions of the disruptor and the incumbent is often documented (Christensen, 1997; Christensen et al., 2015).

Given that the process model considers how the processes initiated by the business-model innovator (i.e., a pioneering cloud-based SaaS provider) interact with the incumbent and other actors, such as customers, partners, media, and so forth, this study reconceptualizes the business-level processes to consist of *the disruptor's and the incumbent's framing.* In the original model, the contextual overlay processes consisted of the strategic and structural context, which make up the context in which change occurs inside the organization (e.g., Gilbert, 2006; Pratap & Saha, 2018). As this study lifts the level of analysis from organizational to ecosystem, there are two contextual aspects: the ecosystems of the disruptor and the incumbent, which are originally separate from each other, but over time coevolve in an interlocking fashion as customers and partners migrate from the incumbent's ecosystem to the disruptor's. Figure 13 maps the activities involved in business-model disruption onto the B–B process model.

Figure 14 illustrates our process model of business-model disruption by depicting the main constructs and the links between them. The first link,

		Actor Response…			
		Actor Level		Ecosystem Level	
		…to Disruptor Framing	…to Incumbent Framing	…to Disruptor's New Ecosystem	…to Incumbent's Old Ecosystem
Force Multiplier	Customers	Resonating	Equivocating	Adopting	Abandoning
	Partners	Resonating	Equivocating	Extending	Abandoning
	Media	Amplifying	Criticizing	Promoting	Demoting
	Analyst	Comparing with Incumbent	Comparing with Disruptor	Comparing with Incumbent's Ecosystem	Comparing with Disruptor's Ecosystem

Figure 13 Ecosystem activities in a process model of business-model disruption

Source: Snihur et al. (2018: 1294).

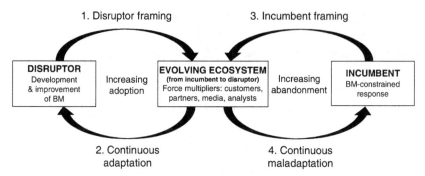

Figure 14 Process model of ecosystem-level business-model disruption dynamics

Source: Snihur et al. (2018: 1292).

a feed-forward process representing the disruptor's framing, connects the disruptor's original business model and the participation of customers, partners, media, and analysts in the emergence of a new, disruptor-centered ecosystem. The second link represents the feedback relationship between the new ecosystem stakeholders' response to the disruptor's framing and the disruptor adapting its business model to the needs of the new ecosystem. This led to an important insight – namely, that the disruptor's framing to the new ecosystem stakeholders and the adaptation of its business model in response to their needs constituted a virtuous framing-adaptation cycle that sustained the increasing adoption of the disruptor's business model. The third link represents the incumbent's framing: a feed-forward process directed to the incumbent's ecosystem stakeholders. The fourth and final link represents the incumbent's maladaptation to the changing ecosystem needs due to constraints from the incumbent's (previously successful) business model. The interplay between the incumbent's framing and the maladaptation of its business model to the changing ecosystem needs constitutes a vicious framing-maladaptation cycle that sustains the increasing abandonment of the incumbent's business model.

The study of Salesforce's framing-adaptation cycle suggests that ecosystem-level interactions play an important role in better capturing business-model disruption dynamics. In doing so, it extends the findings of earlier research that has examined the role of customers (Christensen & Rosenbloom, 1995) and partners (Adner, 2017) by focusing intensely on the interactions of various actors (Gray et al., 2015) during ecosystem evolution. The data suggest that the feed forward and feedback for the disruptor (Figure 14) were amplified by the media, which produced additional raw material, such as various awards, that the disruptor subsequently leveraged to substantiate its leadership.

Researchers have begun to point out the role of external actors, such as media (Pollock & Rindova, 2003; Rao, 1994) or analysts (Beunza & Garud, 2007), as contributors to legitimizing new business models and the new ecosystems formed around them. Their role is important because media and analysts can be "active builders of frames, rather than passive classifiers" (Beunza & Garud, 2007: 22). In our case, it is the disruptor's ability to sustain positive media attention during its early years that might have fueled the dynamics of business-model disruption. Explicitly including these actors in the business-model disruption process model (Figure 14) helps us understand why the disruptor can initiate a virtuous cycle that is difficult for the incumbent to reverse due to the interaction with a variety of actors.

Our process model of evolving ecosystem dynamics (Figure 14) also highlights the importance of *framing* – effective on the part of the disruptor, ineffective on the part of the incumbent – as an important force in shaping ecosystems in addition to patents or licensing fees (Gawer, 2014), standardization of procedures and interfaces (Wareham et al., 2014), the oversight of the quality and number of complementors (Mantovani & Ruiz-Aliseda, 2016), or dynamic control (Dattée et al., 2018). Yet, the framing process contains the seeds of its own destruction: strong framing helps the disruptor shape the ecosystem around its business-model innovation, but over time it might degenerate into a vicious cycle if not accompanied by continuous business-model adaptation by the ecosystem-central firm. For instance, without constant adaptation, firms with central roles in the ecosystem can find themselves diminished or displaced by other ecosystem participants (Adner & Lieberman, 2021). This suggests a somewhat different view of the disruption process than, for instance, the insights of Anderson and Tushman (1990) on technology cycles, which emphasize the importance of the emergence of a dominant design and awareness of technological discontinuities rather than a focus on continuous adaptation and progressive ecosystem shifts.

3.5 Conclusion

This section shows that the B–B process model continues to serve as a useful tool to conceptualize patterns of strategic managerial activities associated with the evolution of large, complex organizations as well as modern business ecosystems. In the evolution of such organizations, new forms labeled as "nonhierarchical," "network," "boundaryless," "virtual," and the like have emerged. Future research based on questions derived from the B–B process model may help shed light on the managerial activities that constitute strategy-making in these and other evolving novel organizational forms.

Analysis based on the B–B process model also suggests that in adaptive organizations, resource allocation and reallocation, and competence deployment and redeployment, are effectively governed by internal selection processes that involve the combined activities of differentially positioned managers. This is why evolutionary theories of the firm must take strategy-making processes seriously, and why resource-based views of the firm must take managerial action seriously. In light of this, network theory and research (Burt, 1992; Hutt et al., 1988), for instance, could help measure strategic context determination and dissolution in terms of growing, or respectively, declining, networks of supporting senior executives in the company over time.

As the recent extension to the ecosystem context illustrates (Snihur et al., 2018), the B–B process model is a potentially useful tool for extending theory about the role of internal selection in organizational evolution to different units and contexts of analysis, such as business models, networks, or ecosystems, where we are still at the start of academic inquiry into the underlying processes and activities (Shipilov & Gawer, 2020; Snihur & Bocken, 2022; Snihur & Eisenhardt, 2022; Thomas et al., 2022).

4 CEO Strategic Leadership and Organizational Evolution

The main premise of the evolutionary approach to strategy-making is that organizational evolution is determined by both the external and internal selection environments of the organization. At the same time, it is also animated by organizational top management, in particular the CEO. The role of the CEO in organizational evolution involves their ability to mediate the dynamic interplay between the firm's external business ecosystem and its internal ecology of strategy-making (see Figure 1). Tool I, presented in Section 2, suggests that strategic leadership of a firm's internal ecology entails two significant processes of simultaneous alignment: (1) of corporate strategy with strategic action and (2) of product-market positioning for competitive advantage with distinctive competences. Both depend on the creation of an internal selection environment capable of timely sensing and adaptation to changes in the external business ecosystem. In this section, we focus specifically on the role of the CEO in organizational evolution.

The five dynamic forces of Tool I delimit the space for the CEO strategic leadership. First, successive CEOs must define the portfolio of businesses in which the firm wants to be a winner, and define what would constitute winning. Second, they must align strategic product-market positioning with the company's distinctive competences to achieve potentially sustainable competitive advantages by creating what customers would perceive as distinct value through related value propositions and business models. Third, they must align strategic action with the announced corporate strategy to realize strategic intent. Fourth, as the relationships between the forces evolve through states of relative harmony, when they are mutually supportive and consistent with each other, and disharmony, when they are not, successive CEOs must realign these forces appropriately in the face of external strategic changes and the corresponding – sometimes inertial – responses of the internal selection environment. However, this leaves us with a relatively static representation of CEO functions and strategy-making practices, which we will try to improve next.

Similarly, existing research about CEOs has usually studied them as chief thinkers and strategy-makers, in line with upper echelons theory (Carpenter et al., 2004; Hambrick, 2007; Hambrick & Mason, 1984). Scholars have documented the relationship between executive personality, cognition, and strategic actions (Barr et al., 1992; Chatterjee & Hambrick, 2007, 2011; Cho & Hambrick, 2006; Crossland et al., 2013; Kaplan, 2008; Nadkarni & Chen, 2014; Yadav et al., 2007). For example, Yadav et al. (2007) showed that CEO attention to the future was associated with the rapidity with which Internet banking was launched. Nadkarni and Chen (2014) generalized the insights of Yadav et al. (2007) by showing that in dynamic environments, new products were introduced more quickly in firms headed by CEOs with low past, high present, and high future focus. They showed that CEOs impacted their firms' innovation and strategic renewal activities through timely leadership.

However, less research has examined longitudinally the relations between successive CEOs and their organization's evolution. A rich CEO succession research has focused on succession antecedents, successor origin (e.g., insider vs. outsider), and relation with firm performance pre- and post-succession (Carpenter et al., 2004; Joshi et al., 2021; Kesner & Sebora, 1994). These studies examine successor-related antecedents such as network embeddedness (Cao et al., 2006) or experience as heir apparent that has been related to lower likelihood of strategic refocusing post-succession (Bigley & Wiersema, 2002). Outsider successors embedded in interfirm social network are typically recommended when strategic renewal is the goal (Cao et al., 2006; Kraatz & Moore, 2002).

Yet, the CEO *strategic leadership* post-succession or the inter-temporal links between successive CEOs remain relatively unexplored. The population of successive CEOs as the unit of observation is seldom studied. As a result, we know little about the ways in which the internal selection environment shaped by a CEO's predecessors constrains an incoming CEO and the ways in which the CEO changes that environment to meet evolving internal and external dynamics. As Das (2004: 58) pointed out, "The temporal dimension deserves comprehensive study because it constitutes a fundamental dimension of strat-egy-making." Our attempts at such a longitudinal examination follow. We highlight these key strategic leadership challenges in two cases: the organiza-tional evolution of HP and the extraordinary case of organizational split, typically initiated by the CEO under conditions of ecosystem bifurcation.

4.1 The CEO and Organizational Evolution

To understand the role and impact of CEO strategic leadership in organization evolution, we begin with the basic idea that no CEO starts with a clean slate and instead must deal with the strategy-making legacy and unresolved strategic challenges of their predecessors. During our study of organizational evolution at HP, we found that successive CEOs shaped the internal selection environment to support the execution of their strategy-making and secure organizational evolution. Specifically, we uncovered three interacting CEO strategy-making practices in service of organizational evolution: (1) harnessing the organiza-tional past; (2) differentially focusing on organizational fit with the current growth trajectories and associated ecosystems and the need (or not) for evol-vability to an extended or new growth trajectory and associated ecosystem; and (3) driving of the organizational future with new strategic intent. The strategic leadership of successive CEOs helped shape HP's organizational evolution, as manifested in changes in the firm's business-model portfolio and distinctive competence over time. These insights are reflected in the framework presented in Figure 15, abstracted from the HP case below, showing CEO-level and organization-level dynamics. The connecting arrows reflect the intricate inter-plays between them.

Each CEO brought with them the experience and track record (at HP or elsewhere) that informed their view of which parts of the past would be important to keep for the future. Each CEO also brought a strategy for how to capitalize on the company's existing growth trajectories (fit) and/or develop new ones (evol-vability), and how to sustain the company's process of evolution through the changes they intended to make in its existing internal selection environment.

At the CEO level of analysis, the above framework indicates how the differential focusing on fit and evolvability practice forms the bridge between the practices of harnessing the past and driving the future during each CEO's tenure, and that all three practices interact. In other words, some CEOs start with a clear strategic intent about driving the future that provides insight into how they need to harness the past and differentially change the focus on fit and evolvability. Others start by harnessing the past, and differentially change the focus on fit or evolvability to drive the future.

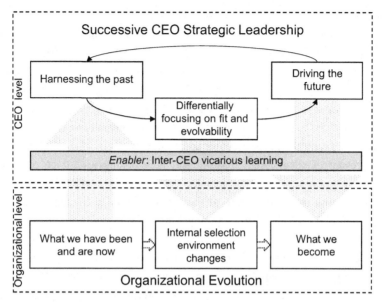

Figure 15 Framework of CEO strategic leadership practices in relation to organizational evolution

Source: Authors.

Inter-CEO vicarious learning helps each successive CEO to exert strategic leadership through the three interacting strategy-making practices and creates interfaces between successive CEOs. The strategic actions of the preceding CEO enable inter-CEO vicarious learning by the succeeding CEO, who learns from the strategic action (or inaction) of their predecessor while developing their own strategic leadership. This inter-CEO-tenure learning is important for CEOs – particularly those who are new to a firm and lack the benefit of insider knowledge. Inter-CEO learning might help CEO adjust more quickly to job requirements in the contemporary times of contracting CEO tenures.

Inter-CEO vicarious learning contrasts with the intra-tenure CEO learning highlighted in previous research (Burgelman, 1988; Henderson et al., 2006). While existing literature suggests the possibility of inter-CEO learning with executive turnover (Virany et al., 1992), it does not systematically document its content. This may be partly because inter-CEO vicarious learning turns out to be a relatively weak process. Our findings indicate that it was not easy for new CEOs to grasp the strategic situation at a company as large and complex as HP. CEO Whitman, for instance, pointed out how difficult it was for her to understand the situation she inherited, despite being an HP board member. Nevertheless, studying inter-CEO vicarious learning sheds additional light on the extent to which successive CEOs read the *not-blank* slate inherited from their predecessors to inform their own strategic leadership to support continued organizational evolution.

At the organizational level of analysis, the framework shows how the changes to the internal selection environment made by the new CEO move the organization from what it had been at the time of CEO transition to what the new CEO wants it to become. To ensure that the internal selection environment served this execution purpose, successive HP CEOs made significant changes to it. These included: (1) centralizing or decentralizing strategic decision-making; (2) allocating resources to different existing and new businesses in the corporate portfolio; (3) emphasis on cost leadership versus spending on R&D for growth; and (4) altering the composition of the top and senior management team to secure alignment with the CEO's strategic intent.

The framework above shows the cycle of CEO-level and organization-level processes of strategy-making and organizational evolution during the tenure of a single CEO. Extending the model into an inter-CEO tenure model turns "What we become" for the incumbent CEO into "What we have been and are now," and therefore the object of the "harnessing the past" practice for the succeeding CEO, thereby starting a new CEO-tenure cycle of strategy-making and organizational evolution. Across these successive cycles, and the strategic legacies they create, each successive CEO challenges the past and envisages the future of the organization in the evolving ecosystem. They use these insights to harness the past pattern of privileging fit or evolvability in resource allocation and drive a new resource allocation pattern that affirms or changes the past one. These within-cycle interplays of CEO strategizing drive the successive modes of adaptation that shape the organization's evolution.

To better reflect these evolutionary dynamics, we extrapolate the frameworks for each individual CEO to a framework incorporating successive CEOs, depicted in Figure 16. This extended framework depicts CEO strategic leadership, incorporating the strategy diamond of each successive CEO (middle of the figure, representing Tool I) as mediating between the evolving ecosystem (top) and the internal ecology of strategy-making (bottom). It reiterates that no CEO starts from a clean slate, but rather must deal with the strategic legacy and unresolved strategic challenges of their predecessors ("harness the past"). That legacy significantly determines the new CEO's initial degree of freedom to develop a corporate strategy to drive the future and continue the process of organizational evolution. Each CEO, in turn, leaves unresolved challenges for their successors.

We represent the interplay between CEO tenures symbolically by showing the overlapping internal ecology, represented by the strategy diamonds (as derived from Tool I, introduced in Section 2) of successive CEOs. After reckoning with the legacy of their predecessors and opening the future with

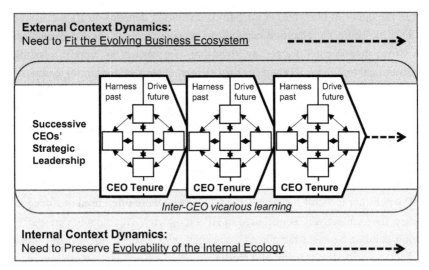

Figure 16 Framework of successive CEO strategic leadership
Source: Adapted from Burgelman et al. (2017: 357).

their own announced strategy, CEOs then close the future through the strategic actions that they take – or fail to take. These strategic actions then become part of the past that the succeeding CEO will have to harness.

Anticipating research into the role of CEO strategic leadership in the process of organizational evolution more than sixty years ago, Philip Selznick distinguished between the "organization" aspect (an expendable rational instrument to do a job) and the "institution" aspect (a responsive, adaptive organism) of social associations (Selznick, 1957: 5–6). Consequently, he also distinguished human interaction-oriented interpersonal leadership from policy-oriented institutional leadership.

Selznick's (1957) seminal analysis of the nature of institutional leadership foreshadowed the important role of CEO strategic leadership for built-to-become organizations. While strategic management researchers have provided evidence of the impact of CEOs on firm innovation and performance, it remains less clear how successive CEO strategic leadership maintains or changes the distinctive character of an organization and its longevity. Our exploratory study of this important question in relation to HP's evolution indicates that the strategic leadership of founders and successive CEOs is fundamental to sustaining the process of organizational evolution.

Interestingly, highlighting the role of strategic leadership in sustaining the process of organizational evolution also sheds additional light on the tension highlighted by Selznick (1957) between instrumental and institutional views of an organization. This tension derives from the reality that a company founded with the intent of becoming a long-lived institution depends on its successive CEOs to secure the adaptive capacity to survive external context dynamics. A strong instrumental orientation, therefore, is necessary to support a lasting institutional orientation. David Packard clearly understood the strategic importance of adopting such an unsentimental perspective if HP was to remain successful in the unforgiving world of business. His efforts to continue to guide his CEO successors informed by this understanding is his lasting contribution to HP's process of evolution.

Our study of HP CEOs also highlights a divergence between the fates of CEOs and organization-level evolution. While on the personal level, managing HP was rather difficult for successive CEOs, who were often fired or forced to retire, they collectively contributed to HP's longevity. This suggests an underlying conflict between the forces associated with leaders' agency and those associated with determinism and inertia.

4.2 The CEO and Organizational Splits

Long-lived multibusiness firms are complex systems that often englobe distinct business models that involve different ways to create and capture value, implying differences across value-chain activities, customers, and partners. The important question for corporate leaders remains how to correctly determine when the business-model portfolio might need to be reconfigured – for instance, due to changes in the business ecosystem where the firm operates. For instance, changes in the business ecosystem can be leveraged to facilitate the launch of new business models (Hou et al., 2020) or can encourage market entry by competitors (Snihur et al., 2021). To help answer this question and based on our analysis of HP, we have developed another framework that helps to elucidate the evolutionary forces driving the CEO's decision to make a corporate split – that is, to transform the firm into multiple independent, smaller, but more adaptive public companies.

A corporate split results in speciation (Garnsey et al., 2008; Lumsden & Singh, 1990; Singh & Lumsden, 1990), or the creation of several new viable corporate entities from one originating corporation. Speciation, rooted in biology, examines the forces that drive previously integral populations to differentially split into new viable ones as the environment, including technological requirements, changes. Our data suggest that changes occurring in the business ecosystem drove HP's PCs-and-printing and enterprise business models apart, and help explain why the transformational corporate split was necessary to enable the two new corporate "species" to adapt better to their specific business-ecosystem conditions. We thus suggest that incipient speciation can help a firm break out of the inertia of coevolutionary lock-in (Burgelman, 2002a) and strategically renew itself. Building on the more proactive view of divestitures emerging in corporate strategy (Berry, 2010; Karim & Capron, 2016), studying splits as speciation allows a generative perspective on divestitures. In this view, the future of *all* the resulting entities is of concern – rather than conceptualizing divestitures as a way to correct past (over-diversification) mistakes.

We used HP as our primary example given the first author's sixteen years of longitudinal research on the organizational strategy-making and evolution at the firm. Over time, HP successfully entered the product markets for computers, inkjet and laser printers, and networking, exploiting distinct business models. For example, it used the unit-based model for computers; the razor-and-blade model for printers and accessories (i.e., selling the printer with a low margin, while making money on the cartridges); and the consulting model to satisfy the information technology needs of business customers. These business models differ in terms of how revenue is generated, what value proposition is developed, and which customers and partners are involved (Chesbrough & Rosenbloom, 2002). Corporate strategy-making in multibusiness firms involves decisions about managing such, more or less well-integrated, business-model portfolios (Sabatier et al., 2010; Snihur & Tarzijan, 2018).

Our analysis of the HP split, announced in 2014 and executed in 2015 by its then-CEO Meg Whitman, suggests that two dynamic strategic forces propelled by external and internal developments shaped her decision to split based on the increasing cost (driven by rising complexity) and the decreasing benefit (driven by decreasing complementarity) of an integrated business-model portfolio. The exogenous evolution of the business ecosystem, typified by the increasing adoption of mobile communication, social networking, and cloud computing, as well as the increasing speed of execution demanded by customers (i.e., force multipliers), capital-market pressure, and the endogenous lateness of HP in responding to these changes, contributed to the timing of the split in the mid-2010s, when the CEO recognized and acted upon this pressure to split.

This framework also connects to the Figure 14 from the previous Section 3.4 on disruption as it suggests how an incumbent firm, such as HP, which managed several business models in its portfolio at the time, might react to the evolving ecosystem by implementing a radical strategy of portfolio split to preserve its evolvability and maintain ecosystem leadership rather than undergo maladaptation (as observed in the case of Siebel, see Snihur et al., 2018).

The framework in Figure 17 illustrates two drivers of diverging business models at the organization that influenced CEO strategy-making: decreasing inter-business-model complementarity and increasing intra-business-model complexity. Both drivers are impacted by the evolving business ecosystem.

Figure 17 Framework of corporate split drivers
Source: Burgelman et al. (2022b: 17).

The first dimension, *inter-business-model complementarity*, refers to the degree to which respective products, customers, partners, and underlying technology can benefit from the presence of additional business models in the corporate portfolio. In other words, the existence of inter-business-model complementarity suggests that there are collaboration opportunities between the firm's business models, and synergies can result from exploiting these existing complementarities. As an example, at HP, similar components were used for PCs and enterprise servers, allowing back-office collaboration in sourcing between the two business models and stronger bargaining power vis-à-vis the firm's suppliers, enabled by HP's integrated operation of two different business models in its portfolio.

Increasing inter-business-model complementarity is a useful strategic force to understand the success of today's diversified firms, such as Google or Amazon. Digitalization and platformization, combined with artificial intelligence (AI) and machine learning (ML) from large swathes of data, create opportunities for new business models and cross-boundary disruptions to augment product- or component-derived complementarities, which were the main source of complementarities in the past. These technological advances extend corporate strategic leadership capability to effectively support an enlarged business-model portfolio by augmenting inter-business-model complementarity. However, inter-business-model complementarity can also decrease – for instance, due to the bifurcation of evolving business ecosystems. This happened in the case of HP when personal and enterprise computing began to bifurcate in late 2000s.

The second dimension in our framework is *intra-business-model complexity*. In line with Simon's (1962: 468) definition of complexity in a system as "a large number of parts that interact in a non-simple way," intra-business-model complexity is generated by a high number of activities, customers, and partners;

technological sophistication; and the interdependencies between them within business models. Intra-business-model complexity makes high demands on managerial information processing and attention capabilities. For instance, at HP, the shift of computing to the cloud in late 2000s significantly increased the complexity of activities and the number of partners involved in the firm's enterprise consulting business model.

When inter-business-model complementarity is high and intra-business-model complexity is low, there is no need to reconfigure the corporate portfolio and the company is better keeping all its constitutive parts "together." As inter-business-model complementarity decreases (while intra-business-model complexity stays low), pursuing strategic integration becomes harder because executives, managers, and employees within the company find it more difficult to define jointly attractive cross-business opportunities.

For example, in the case of HP, this meant that collaboration opportunities between the PC, printing, and enterprise consulting business models became harder for corporate managers to spot and quickly execute. In the medium to long term, this situation jeopardizes corporate survival chances due to the lack of renewal opportunities in an ever-evolving environment, particularly a highly dynamic one faced by HP. This lack of collaboration can eventually result in divestment, just as IBM successively divested its printer, PC, and semiconductor businesses. Other recent examples of splits include GE, GSK, Johnson & Johnson, Siemens, and Toshiba.

As intra-business-model complexity increases (while inter-business-model complementarity stays high), the evaluation of new opportunities becomes challenging. This is because it becomes more difficult for executives, managers, and employees to understand, support, and evaluate multiple complex business strategies and associated resource requirements, particularly regarding the extension of corporate strategy to new technological frontiers of their product markets. This difficulty is due to executives' bounded rationality and imagination, and computational problems related to cognitively and behaviorally dealing with increasing complexity.

In the HP case, this meant that spotting and implementing radical innovative technologies, such as 3D printing for the printing business-model or cloud-based solutions for the Internet of Things within the enterprise consulting business model, became more challenging under conditions of increasing intra-business-model complexity. High intra-business-model complexity also provides a potentially helpful explanation for Google's and Microsoft's previously unsuccessful efforts to develop health-care-related businesses, as those were characterized by extreme complexity. In the medium to long term, this situation jeopardizes corporate survival due to reduced corporate renewal when the organization is no longer capable of processing external signals about its environment and adapting to evolving circumstances.

Simultaneously decreasing inter-business-model complementarity and increasing intra-business-model complexity within a business-model port-folio therefore impose limits on corporate strategic leadership's capability to keep the organization whole and well-functioning. Such simultaneous and interacting forces increase internal pressure (from managers and employees) and external pressure (from capital markets and investors) to formalize the diverging business models through a decision to scale down – that is, split the company into independent and smaller constitutive parts. Such a decision is most often undertaken by the top strategic leader: the organiza-tion's CEO.

In the case of HP, the exogenous evolution and growth of cloud computing and mobile communications, and the endogenous lateness of HP in recognizing the importance of these changes, contributed to decreasing inter-business-model complementarity and increasing intra-business-model complexity in its business-model portfolio, intensifying pressure to reconfigure the firm's port-folio by splitting the company. The effects of the two forces are not simply additive; they also amplify each other, as increasing complexity makes it much harder to leverage complementarity benefits.

Our framework suggests that some CEOs might be better at detecting when the timing for the split is right. In the case of Whitman, she was an outsider with less emotional commitment to keeping HP together and an excellent strategist. Existing research has criticized short-tenured outsider CEOs for underappre-ciating interdependencies in legacy business divestitures (Feldman, 2014). We suggest, however, that skillful outsider CEOs might be ideally qualified for undertaking corporate splits, as they can interpret and articulate organizational business-model divergence and ecosystem bifurcation and are the ultimate decision-makers activating the corporate split.

Our split framework also suggests that a company's size per se is a static concept and not necessarily always the source of economies of scope or the best way to evaluate company performance and prospects, especially in cases when the company manages a portfolio of diverse business models. Applying this insight to the case of HP leads to the conclusion that, at certain points in the process of organizational evolution, it may be better to reduce the size of the company than try to increase it.

We term this problem *organizational fragility*, defined as a greater downside than upside potential associated with corporate scale and scope. Organizational fragility at HP meant greater negative than positive potential in its adaptive capacity associated with the diverging adaptive requirements of its PC, printing, and enterprise consulting business models. This organizational fragility arose because top management's ability to manage the diverging business-model portfolio was increasingly thinly stretched. By 2015 the strategic integration challenges had outgrown HP's corporate-level strategic leadership capability, and the company was now pursuing overambitious strategic integration efforts that would drive it inexorably toward reduced adaptive capacity. After the HP split was finalized in 2015, both the resulting companies were half the size of the presplit HP, which fostered a significantly narrower corporate strategy at each firm and provided clearer and speedier ways to pursue new opportunities.

Our evolutionary approach suggests that there are moments during the corporate trajectory when it becomes clear that the company is being overambitious about the strategic integration of diverging business models within its portfolio. This can exacerbate organizational fragility, where the upside from integrating different business models in a corporate portfolio is minimal, threatening long-term survival. At times like these, adaptive portfolio reconfiguration might be warranted, in order to reduce organizational fragility and enable renewal through radically splitting the organization into smaller entities.

4.3 Conclusion

The analysis offered in this section suggests that strategy-making in organizations should be viewed as an open-ended evolutionary process that does not depend on the ex ante teleological vision of any given corporate leader. To sustain the company's evolution, each successive CEO must be able to act as an agent who links the company's close-ended past and its open-ended future. This, in turn, requires analyzing how the internal ecology of strategy-making, driven by the strategic leadership of successive CEOs in relation to the company's evolving ecosystem, shapes the composition of the company's business-model portfolio and its various induced or autonomous strategic initiatives.[8]

Considering this, our analysis also revealed that a particular CEO in that evolving process may recognize that the company has reached a point of singularity at which it is clear that the company's ecosystem and business-model portfolio have inexorably bifurcated, and that it is no longer possible to determine a viable corporate strategy for the company. This then requires a corporate portfolio split and the "speciation" of smaller, independent new entities, each more adaptive to its differentiated ecosystem.

---

[8] For practitioner-focused approaches to such analyses, see Snihur et al. (2022) for a structured analytical approach to understanding business model portfolio trajectories, and Iyer and Basole (2016) and Basole et al. (2016) for ecosystem visualization and decision support.

5 Toward a Theory of Strategy-Making and Organizational Evolution

This final section recapitulates the foundational conceptual frameworks for consolidating the theory of strategy-making in organizational evolution and positions that theory within the academic discipline of strategic management (Section 5.1). We also discuss methodological and theoretical implications (Section 5.2) and suggest directions for future research (Section 5.3), setting the stage for the Epilogue.

5.1 Foundational Conceptual Frameworks of Strategy-Making

Perhaps the most important contribution of the evolutionary perspective consists in showing that the internal ecology of strategy-making – and the associated internal selection environment – is an emergent property of organizations (Section 2). This emergent aspect depends on strategy-making as featured particularly in the process models of ICV, SBE, and CVC (Section 3). These process models also explain how novelty can emerge and how organizations can renew and adapt from within. Furthermore, the research findings show that this strategic renewal process may be strongly influenced by the approach of the CEO and top management team during any period of the company's evolution (Section 4). The various tools presented in the preceding sections are valuable for managerial practice to develop firm strategy at the CEO level, as well as to understand and participate in strategy-making at the operational and middle-management levels of the organization.

5.1.1 Internal Ecology of Organizational Strategy-Making

The internal ecology model – the major focus of Section 2 – views organization-level strategy as the result of successful strategic initiatives of interdependent actors (individuals or groups), who can commit the organization and who continuously try to do so. In this model, strategy-making is a highly dynamic process that capitalizes on anticipated and unanticipated variations in the internal and external environments and their implications for the firm's business model(s). It views the strategy-making process as constituting an opportunity structure for strategic leaders in the organization, but one in which individual opportunity seeking is constrained, to some extent, by the imperative of organizational survival. This model is probably most effective in highly uncertain, opportunity-rich environments. Coherence of system-level strategic action depends on the characteristics of the internal selection environment – although the power of the CEO to initiate large-scale changes, such as splitting the organization, is also a factor (Section 4). The internal ecology of strategy-making can be fruitfully related to other (complementary) theoretical approaches in strategic management.

5.1.2 Emergent and Deliberate Strategy

It is important to keep levels of analysis clearly in mind when discussing the link between induced and autonomous strategy-making processes in the internal ecology model and *emergent and deliberate strategies* (Mintzberg, 1978). Induced and deliberate strategies are similar, but the induced strategy process provides more detail on what is involved in getting the organization to implement corporate strategy. The link with autonomous strategic initiatives, on the other hand, is more complicated. Autonomous initiatives involved in generating and developing a new business opportunity usually involve deliberate actions taken by leaders at levels of the organization below top management. These leaders' actions nurture new competencies or business models, helping to create a new strategic position that may open up a new business opportunity for the corporation. Thus, a strategy that is emergent at the level of the corporation often has its roots in deliberate actions at lower levels. Similarly, variations that are unplanned from the company's perspective may be planned from the perspective of the lower-level leaders who engage in them. Even unsuccessful autonomous initiatives – "ephemeral" ones (Mirabeau & Maguire, 2014) – may nevertheless have important impacts on how the organization develops its dynamic capabilities (Burgelman, 2002b; Keil et al., 2009).

5.1.3 Guided Evolution

Lovas and Ghoshal (2000) reported a case study of a Danish company that suggested to the authors the possibility of organizational evolution "guided" by top management. In some ways, guided evolution suggests the possibility of inducing autonomous strategic action, which brings it back more closely to the traditional rational-actor model of strategy-making. Since we define autonomous strategic initiatives in terms of their difference from the product-market and competency categories encompassed by the corporate strategy, top management can of course initiate autonomous strategic initiatives. However, as the study of Andy Grove's strategic leadership at Intel indicates (Burgelman, 2002a), top management is likely to impose the logic of the existing corporate strategy on such autonomous initiatives (inertia I), or to become rapidly impatient and emaciate the strategic context determination process (inertia II). Figure 18 illustrates these two forms of strategic inertia, building on Tool II from Figure 2.

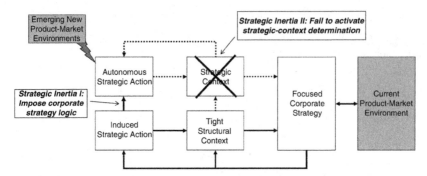

Figure 18 Inertial effects of a strategy vector on the internal ecology
of strategy-making

Source: Adapted from Burgelman (2002a).

Also, top management may "forget" that the initiative emerged from below
and claim ownership of its initiation if it is successful retrospectively
(Burgelman, 2016). For instance, whereas Steve Jobs reportedly told his biog-
rapher that he asked his team to come up with a multi-touch screen, Jonathan
Ive, the team leader, had a different memory of the development:

> He said his design team had already been working on a multi-touch input that
> was developed for the trackpads of Apple's MacBook Pro, and they were
> experimenting with ways to transfer that capability to a computer screen. They
> used a projector to show on a wall what it would look like. "This is going to
> change everything," Ive told his team. But he was careful not to show it to Jobs
> right away, especially since his people were working on it in their spare time and
> he didn't want to squash their enthusiasm. "Because Steve is so quick to give an
> opinion, I don't show him stuff in front of other people," Ive recalled. "He might
> say, 'This is shit,' and snuff the idea. (. . .)." (Isaacson, 2011: 468)

5.1.4 Ambidextrous Organizations

Ambidextrous organizations (O'Reilly & Tushman, 2011; Raisch &
Birkinshaw, 2008; Simsek, 2009; Tushman & O'Reilly, 1997) are capable of
handling both incremental and revolutionary change. The idea is closely related
to the framework of induced and autonomous strategy processes, but there are
two important differences. First, induced and autonomous initiatives do not
necessarily map on to incremental and radical technological change. Change in
the induced strategy process, while nominally "incremental," can still be very
large. For instance, developing a new airframe is incremental for Boeing (the
next step after the 787), but still costs billions of dollars. In the induced strategy
process, "incremental" simply means change that is well understood – doing

more of what the company already knows how to do well. Change through the autonomous process, on the other hand, can be "radical," but is usually rather small at first. However, it always involves doing things that are unfamiliar to the company – doing what it is not sure it can do well. Second, change through the autonomous strategy process usually comes about fortuitously and unexpectedly, and senior and top management embark on it without any clear understanding of its strategic importance for the company and how it relates to the company's distinctive competencies and capabilities. Resolving this indeterminacy is the most difficult challenge facing autonomous strategic initiatives. This highlights the importance of the strategic context determination process.

5.2 Methodological and Theoretical Implications

Our longitudinal grounded research methods (discussed in the Preface) have generated conceptual frameworks that stand between the narratives of historical science and the mathematical/statistical models of reductionist social science (Burgelman, 2011; Gaddis, 2002). We have shown that such frameworks are useful to conceptualize substantive areas of strategy-making in large, complex organizations that involve multiple levels of management both sequentially *and* simultaneously. They help "identify the relevant variables and the questions that the user must answer in order to develop conclusions" (Spender & Kraaijenbrink, 2011: 52). However, they cannot resolve the uncertainty – the "objective ignorance" (Kahneman et al., 2021: 144–147) – associated with strategic issues and the challenges facing strategy-making. Nevertheless, if "models do better than people, but not by much … Still better is good, and models are better" (Kahneman et al., 2021: 147), we suggest that the value of developing frameworks based on longitudinal grounded research should be assessed, at least in part, in terms of their ability to help other scholars develop better models in further research (see also Firestein, 2016) and advance process research in strategic management (Kouamé & Langley, 2018).

5.2.1 Managerial Action in Strategy-Making

In Section 3, we identified the multilevel interlocking activities involved in the process models of ICV, SBE, CVC, and ecosystem-level business-model disruption. Identifying such networks of interlocking multilevel managerial activities in other substantive areas – such as strategic acquisition integration, strategic partnerships, and strategic globalization (or deglobalization) decisions – would provide further insight into managerial action in strategy-making, bringing the study of managers even more forcefully into research programs of strategic management and organizational evolution. Such research could complement studies of top management teams (cf. Steffensen et al., 2019), middle management (e.g., Mantere, 2008; Wooldridge et al., 2008), and functional managers (Menz & Scheef, 2014) in the extant strategic management research.

We also showed the graphical linking and sequencing of the different types of these interlocking multilevel managerial activities, which suggest it would be interesting to show the dynamics of how these processes play out over time with the help of behavioral and/or computer simulations. This could shed further light, for instance, on how the dynamics of process models of different substantive areas of strategy-making might differ in organizations with functional, product, geography, matrix, or other types of structures. This could provide deeper insight into the behavioral, cognitive, emotional, internal organizational, and external ecosystem forces that facilitate or impede the effective performance of these complex processes.

5.2.2 CEO Leadership in Strategy-Making

In Section 4, we introduced topics related to the role of CEO strategic leadership and its connections to organizational evolution. This analysis helps us reconcile tensions between continuity and change in organizational evolution by bringing the issue of CEO legacy to the fore. Researchers have suggested that "bringing the past into the present can be as complex and comprehensive as directing the present toward the future" (Hatch & Schultz, 2017: 35). We show how this tension between past and future can be balanced by successive CEOs through tailored integration of past and future into the internal ecology of strategy-making.

Our frameworks from this section reassert the fundamental importance of the CEO in mediating the interplay of the business ecosystem and internal ecology (potentially constituted by multiple business models, cf. Aversa et al., 2021; Khanagha et al., 2014) by acting as the custodian of the organization's past and simultaneously the catalyst (or reactant)'for its future. Prior research has shown how organizational members' bottom-up rethinking of the past, reconsidering of the present, and reimagining of the future must fit together to enable strategic transformation (Kaplan & Orlikowski, 2013) or new product development (Hatch & Schultz, 2017; Ravasi et al., 2019). For example, Hatch and Schultz (2017) have documented how the past resurfaced through a bottom-up initiative at Carlsberg. The lack of CEO support for these initiatives might explain why these scholars find that organizational heritage has a certain characteristic of latency.

Our work suggests that lingering organizational legacy needs to be reactivated by the CEO and transferred to the organization to sustain its evolution over time. For instance, founder novelty orientation (Snihur & Zott, 2020) originating with Hewlett and Packard themselves was reactivated at HP by Young, and later by Whitman. On the other hand, new CEOs, especially when coming from outside the organization, might make changes to signify how their strategic leadership regime differs from their predecessor's, as Fiorina did at HP. Those parts of the legacy not taken up by subsequent CEOs, however, can atrophy or be forgotten, implying interesting further research opportunities about tracing organizational evolution in cultural, cognitive, and behavioral terms.

Counter to the prevailing views of CEOs as semi-heroic figures paid enormous salaries to steer organizations to create shareholder value (Mizruchi & Marshall, 2016), or as narcissists emboldened by social praise (Chatterjee & Hambrick, 2007, 2011), our analysis suggests that CEOs are under considerable pressure to learn fast (from their predecessors) and to harness the lingering past to drive the organizational future (cf Figure 1).

5.2.3 Business Models and Ecosystems in Strategy-Making

Our work suggests that business models provide an important unit of analysis to understand organizational evolution and might play a role in the selection processes within large complex organizations. Although rarely considered in the context of evolutionary theory or corporate strategy, business-model innovation has been examined mostly from the point of view of new, often disruptive entrants (Garud et al., 2022; Martins et al., 2015; McDonald & Eisenhardt, 2020; Zuzul & Tripsas, 2020; see Snihur & Eisenhardt, 2022 for a review). Existing business models can be a source of maladaptation to the evolving ecosystem, as in the case of Siebel's maladaptation to the SaaS business model of Salesforce (Snihur et al., 2018; Figure 14) or in the case of digitalization of newspapers (Cozzolino & Verona, in press; Gilbert, 2005). Our research suggests that the analysis of business models can lead to decisions about corporate split as documented in the case of HP (Burgelman et al., 2022; Snihur et al., 2022; Figure 17) and business models can be a source of organizational renewal through such splits by providing additional sources for focused experimentation (Bocken & Snihur, 2020; McDonald & Eisenhardt, 2020).

Our work also suggests connections between different elements of the organizational world during evolution processes. For example, our framework of disruptive innovation (Section 3.4) shows the connections between organizational strategies related to business-model innovation and ecosystem-level dynamics as the ecosystem evolves in favor of the disruptor. Our framework of corporate split (Section 4.2) connects the evolving ecosystem with diverging business models at the organization level and the CEO's strategy-making at the individual (top) manager level. In particular, our work suggests that not only do CEOs shape their organizations, but through strategic action and language they can also seek to shape their ecosystems (Section 4.2). This complements emerging ecosystem research into the managerial capabilities that are important for sensing (Helfat & Peteraf, 2015) and reside at the level of the individual top manager (Adner & Helfat, 2003; Ethiraj & Levinthal, 2004; Helfat & Martin, 2015).

However, such strong shaping, or vectoring, can also result in coevolutionary lock-in, as became the case of Intel under CEO Grove (Burgelman, 2002a). Thus, a fundamental insight is that "shaping" an ecosystem is potentially a double-edged evolutionary sword. Additionally, such frameworks help push the boundaries of current understanding of organizational processes through cross-level recursive loops and multilevel theorizing that strengthen the foundations of organizational evolution theory of strategic management with process insights (Burgelman et al., 2018).

This research thus augments current perspectives on ecosystems (Adner, 2017; Ansari et al., 2016; Dattée et al., 2018; Jacobides et al., 2018; Thomas & Ritala, 2022) and business models (Amit & Zott, 2001; Lanzolla & Markides, 2021; Leppänen et al., in press; Snihur & Eisenhardt, 2022; Snihur & Zott, 2020) by connecting conversations about the external and internal organizational environment to actual processes that determine organizational evolution and longevity, as well as CEO strategizing. Existing perspectives have tended to take either value-oriented competitive (e.g., Adner, 2017; Amit & Zott, 2001) or technology-oriented innovation (e.g., Jacobides et al., 2018; Teece, 2010) approaches to both ecosystem and business models research.

In contrast, the evolutionary lens is new to both the ecosystem and business-model literatures, which have evolved relatively separately during the last decade and are still in need of additional theoretical underpinnings. Our frameworks, connecting the disruptor's business-model innovation with ecosystem change (Section 3.4), the CEO's mediating role between the internal selection environment and the ecosystem (Section 4.1, Figure 1), and theorizing organizational response to ecosystem bifurcation through the split of business-model portfolio (Section 4.2) bring a fresh perspective on the potential of these literatures to coevolve (pun intended). We also suggest that the CEO might occupy a crucial position as a mediator between external ecosystem dynamics and internal, often business-model-related processes. The CEO level of analysis remains little studied in either the ecosystem or business-model literature, and further investigation is needed.

5.2.4 Organizational Path Dependence and Path Creation

Our work also has implications for our understanding of path dependence and path creation. Path dependence occurs when an end state depends on a particular sequence of unfolding events (Arthur, 1989; David, 1985; Garud & Karnoe, 2001). Our process models suggest the ways in which previous events shape the evolution of organization, and the role of the CEO in this process. Another way of thinking about the CEO's role is *path creation* (Garud et al., 2010), in the sense that the CEO can meaningfully navigate the path even as they are creating it (Garud & Karnoe, 2001). However, little research has systematically considered how path dependence created by a CEO predecessor potentially constrains the path creation of the CEO successor, and how path creation, in turn, shapes the internal selection environment facing the next CEO.

5.3 Future Research Directions

The insights produced by the evolutionary lens link the theory of strategy-making more closely to evolutionary organization theory and provide several avenues for cumulative knowledge development. Further research, for instance, could focus on the characteristics of the internal selection environment that are associated with high adaptiveness – or, conversely, engender inertial tendencies in established companies. Future studies could also focus on the role of strategic context determination and dissolution processes in helping established companies cope with internal and external variation and associated dilemmas identified by research in organizational ecology and the economic theory of the firm. Further study of the leadership activities that constitute these processes, and of the external and internal forces that shape them, offers the prospect of adding meaningfully to the knowledge base that can strengthen the strategic leadership capability of large, complex organizations. Additionally, scholars have only just begun to examine the intricate processes involved in ecosystem bifurcation and corporate splits, and their implications for organizations and their strategy-making. Increasing dynamism, regulatory, climate, and technological changes suggest a need for additional research in this direction, as many organizations need to adapt to ecosystem evolution and pressing environmental concerns.

Our work has implications for research on the role of CEO strategic leadership in evolving organizations. First, we identify successive CEOs as a novel unit of observation for organization scholars, suggesting a need for additional studies examining CEO populations rather than only the impact of individual CEOs. Second, as noted earlier, Selznick's (1957) seminal analysis of the nature of institutional leadership foreshadowed the important role of CEO strategic leadership for built-to-become organizations. While strategic management researchers have provided evidence of the impact of CEOs on firm innovation and performance, it is not yet clear how successive CEO strategic leadership maintains or changes the distinctive character of an organization and sustains its longevity. Our exploratory study of this important question in relation to HP's evolution indicates that the strategic leadership of founders and successive CEOs is fundamental to sustaining the process of organizational evolution. However, future comparative research into the sustaining and nonsustaining processes of organizational evolution is necessary to gain further insight into the consequences of interfaces between CEO legacy and the efforts of new CEOs to renew the organization and sustain its evolution. For instance, our research points to the important role of inter-CEO vicarious learning, and further research could explore the factors that determine the relative strength of this inter-CEO learning process, and whether and how it could be augmented – for instance, through machine-generated learning algorithms.

Our work also highlights a divergence between the fates of CEOs and organization-level evolution. While managing HP was a tough personal challenge for successive CEOs, together they contributed to HP's longevity. This suggests an underlying conflict between forces associated with leadership and forces associated with determinism and inertia. More research focused on examining the interface between individual-level leadership, CEOs' career imperatives, and evolutionary organization-level challenges would be valuable.

Business models offer an additional level of analysis to help focus on organizational learning problems (e.g., due to increasing complexity when running several business models in parallel), as is also highlighted in such recent approaches as the lean start-up (Bocken & Snihur, 2020; Ries, 2011) or the strong focus on learning in the development of AI. How organizations can learn well and quickly – for instance, using experiments and algorithms in real time, facilitated by digitalization and the increasing ease of data collection – remains an important problem to ensure organizational adaptation and longevity in turbulent environments.

We hope that the tools and frameworks set out in this Element provide a firm foundation for further development of the evolutionary theory of organizational strategy-making, particularly considering strategy-making in this process.

Epilogue: Toward a New Strategy-Making "Technostructure" Governed by Artificial Intelligence and Machine Learning?

The preceding sections of our Element have affirmed the critical role of managerial agency in animating the internal ecology of strategy-making that interacts with the evolving ecosystem and shapes the evolution of complex organizations. They indicate that the decisions and action imperatives facing *strategic* leaders in such organizations are typically not well structured and lend themselves less well to quantitative methods that help solve well-structured managerial problems. Today's rapid technological advances associated with AI – especially artificial general intelligence (AGI) – and ML, however, sometimes seem to promise the possibility of reducing the critical role of strategic leadership and deserve to be considered, at least briefly, as we complete our intellectual journey.

We began our journey through the study of strategy-making in organizational evolution with the first author's (1969) licentiate thesis at Antwerp University, which was strongly informed by Chandler (1962), Penrose (1959), and Ansoff (1965). As our voyage draws to a close, therefore, it is interesting to mention that his thesis was also informed by John Kenneth Galbraith's *The New Industrial State* (1967). Galbraith described how a relatively small number of massively large corporations formed a new "industrial system." Associated with this, he saw the rise of a corporate "technostructure" that "embraces all who bring specialized knowledge, talent or experience to group decision-making. This, not the management, is the guiding intelligence – the brain – of the enterprise" (p. 71). The rise of the technostructure implied that the role of management had basically changed from substantive decision-making to ratification.

Ironically, while Galbraith's technostructure did not turn out to be quite as dominant as envisaged in 1967, in 2022 some scholars appear to believe that a new type of technostructure may already exert significant influence in corporate strategy-making. For instance, Jacobides et al. (2021) have recently investigated the complex interdependency patterns that connect the developers, manufacturers, and users of AI and ML. By distinguishing between AI enablement, AI production, and AI consumption, they analyze the emerging patterns of specialization between firms and communities and find that AI provision is characterized by the dominance of a small number of Big Tech firms, whose downstream use of AI (e.g., in online search, payments, and social media) has underpinned much of the recent progress in AI, and who also provide the necessary upstream computing power (through platforms such as Cloud and Edge). Furthermore, they also find that these same firms dominate in supporting top academic institutions in AI research, further strengthening their own position.

So, looking forward, it seems appropriate to ask whether a new and more powerful nonhuman technostructure is now truly on the verge of reducing the role of managerial agency from substantive strategic decision-making to mere ratification. Expert views provide only tentative and somewhat ambiguous guidance for answering this fundamental question. Some computer scientists explain why current AI is excellent for solving relatively narrow strategies for well-defined games such as chess, Go, and Jeopardy, but also explain why it will be difficult to attain AGI because machines are unlikely to be able to master the abductive reasoning capability associated with the human mind (e.g., Larson, 2021). Others (e.g., Kissinger et al., 2021: 212), however, more radically foresee that AGI will be able to learn and execute a broad range of tasks, just as humans do, and raise strategic questions such as " ... [w]ho controls AGI? ... [w]hat does partnership with AI look like?," or what AGI might mean for the future of organizational structure and hierarchical organization (Ojanperä & Vuori, 2021).

Still others adopt a pragmatic approach, informed by behavioral research. As Kahneman et al. (2021: 146) put it: "As long as algorithms are not nearly perfect – and, in many domains, objective ignorance dictates that they will never be – human judgement will not be replaced. That is why it must be improved." Their conclusion implies the need for further research into how AI and ML may help humans improve their judgment, but without such judgment being reduced to ratification of AI/ML-determined strategic decisions.

This, then, is where we end our journey. As we write, strategic management research stands at the threshold of a new area of knowledge: how decision-makers might integrate the judgments of people and machines. We have come a long way in our understanding of strategy-making processes, but it is clear that we still have much to learn. Because whatever the future may bring, in terms of organizations and the minds – whether human or otherwise – that direct them, one thing is certain: our analytical tools must be fit for the task.

References

Adner, R. 2017. Ecosystem as structure: An actionable construct for strategy. *Journal of Management*, 43(1): 39–58.

Adner, R., & Helfat, C. E. 2003. Corporate effects and dynamic managerial capabilities. *Strategic Management Journal*, 24(10): 1011–1025.

Adner, R., & Kapoor, R. 2010. Value creation in innovation ecosystems: How the structure of technological interdependence affects firm performance in new technology generations. *Strategic Management Journal*, 31(3): 306–333.

Adner, R., & Lieberman, M. 2021. Disruption through complements. *Strategy Science*, 6(1): 91–109.

Aldrich, H. E. 1979. *Organizations and environments*. Englewood Cliffs, NJ: Prentice-Hall.

Aldrich, H. E. 1999. *Organizations evolving*. London: Sage.

Allison, G., & Zelikow, P. 1999. *Essence of decision: Explaining the cuban missile crisis* (2nd ed.). New York: Pearson PTE.

Amit, R., & Zott, C. 2001. Value creation in e-business. *Strategic Management Journal*, 22(6–7): 493–520.

Anderson, P., & Tushman, M. L. 1990. Technological discontinuities and dominant designs: A cyclical model of technological change. *Administrative Science Quarterly*, 35(4): 604–633.

Ansari, S., Garud, R., & Kumaraswamy, A. 2016. The disruptor's dilemma: TiVo and the U.S. television ecosystem. *Strategic Management Journal*, 37(9): 1829–1853.

Ansoff, H. I. 1965. *Corporate strategy: An analytic approach to business policy for growth and expansion*. New York: McGraw-Hill.

Arthur, W. B. 1989. Competing technologies, increasing returns, and lock-in by historical events. *The Economic Journal*, 99(394): 116–131.

Aversa, P., Haefliger, S., Hueller, F., & Reza, D. G. 2021. Customer complementarity in the digital space: Exploring Amazon's business model diversification. *Long Range Planning*, 54(5): 101985.

Barnett, W. P., Greve, H. R., & Park, D. Y. 1994. An evolutionary model of organizational performance. *Strategic Management Journal*, 15: 11–28.

Barney, J. 1991. Firm resources and sustained competitive advantage. *Journal of Management*, 17(1): 99–120.

Barr, P. S., Stimpert, J. L., & Huff, A. S. 1992. Cognitive change, strategic action, and organizational renewal. *Strategic Management Journal*, 13: 15–36.

Basole, R. C., Huhtamäki, J., Still, K., & Russell, M. G. 2016. Visual decision support for business ecosystem analysis. *Expert Systems with Applications*, 65: 271–282.

Berry, H. 2010. Why do firms divest? *Organization Science*, 21(2): 380–396.

Beunza, D., & Garud, R. 2007. Calculators, lemmings or frame-makers? The intermediary role of securities analysts. *The Sociological Review*, 55(2_suppl): 13–39.

Bigley, G. A., & Wiersema, M. F. (2002). New CEOs and corporate strategic refocusing: How experience as heir apparent influences the use of power. *Administrative Science Quarterly*, 47(4): 707–727.

Bocken, N., & Snihur, Y. 2020. Lean startup and the business model: Experimenting for novelty and impact. *Long Range Planning*, 53(4): 101953.

Bogers, M., Chesbrough, H., & Moedas, C. 2018. Open innovation: Research, practices, and policies. *California Management Review*, 60(2): 5–16.

Bower, J. L. 1970. *Managing the resource allocation process: A study of corporate planning and investment*. Boston, MA: Harvard Business School Press.

Boyd, R., & Richerson, P. J. 1985. *Culture and the evolutionary process*. Chicago, IL: University of Chicago Press.

Burgelman, R. A. 1969. *Optimale grootte in bedrijfseconomisch perspectief*. Licenciate Thesis, Faculty of Applied Economics, Antwerp University (UFSIA), Antwerp.

Burgelman, R. A. 1980. *Managing innovating systems: A study of the process of internal corporate venturing*. New York: Columbia University.

Burgelman, R. A. 1983a. Corporate entrepreneurship and strategic management: Insights from a process study. *Management Science*, 29(12): 1349–1364.

Burgelman, R. A. 1983b. A model of the interaction of strategic behavior, corporate context, and the concept of strategy. *Academy of Management Review*, 8(1): 61–70.

Burgelman, R. A. 1983c. A process model of internal corporate venturing in the diversified major firm. *Administrative Science Quarterly*, 28(2): 223–244.

Burgelman, R. A. 1984. Managing the internal corporate venturing process. *MIT Sloan Management Review*, 25(2): 33–48.

Burgelman, R. A. 1985. Managing the new venture division: Research findings and implications for strategic management. *Strategic Management Journal*, 6(1): 39–54.

Burgelman, R. A. 1988. Strategy making as a social learning process: The case of internal corporate venturing. *Journal on Applied Analytics*, 18(3): 74–85.

Burgelman, R. A. 1990. Strategy-making and organizational ecology: A conceptual integration. In J. V. Singh (Ed.), *Organizational evolution: New directions*: 164–181. Newbury Park, CA: Sage.

Burgelman, R. A. 1991. Intraorganizational ecology of strategy making and organizational adaptation: Theory and field research. *Organization Science*, 2(3): 239–262.

Burgelman, R. A. 1994. Fading memories: A process theory of strategic business exit in dynamic environments. *Administrative Science Quarterly*, 39(1): 24–56.

Burgelman, R. A. 1996. A process model of strategic business exit: Implications for an evolutionary perspective on strategy. *Strategic Management Journal*, 17(S1): 193–214.

Burgelman, R. A. 2002a. Strategy as vector and the inertia of coevolutionary lock-in. *Administrative Science Quarterly*, 47(2): 325–357.

Burgelman, R. A. 2002b. *Strategy is destiny: How strategy-making shapes a company's future.* New York: The Free Press.

Burgelman, R. A. 2011. Bridging history and reductionism: A key role for longitudinal qualitative research. *Journal of International Business Studies*, 42(5): 591–601.

Burgelman, R. A. 2016. Built to become: HP's history of becoming 1939–2016: An integral process overview. Stanford Research Paper Series 3273, Stanford Business School.

Burgelman, R. A., Snihur, Y., & Thomas, L. D. (2022). Why multibusiness corporations split: CEO strategizing as the ecosystem evolves. *Journal of Management*, 48(7): 2108–2151.

Burgelman, R. A., Cogan, G. W., & Graham, B. K. 1997. Strategic business exit and corporate transformation: Evolving links of technology strategy and substantive and generic corporate strategies. In H. Chesbrough, & R. A. Burgelman (Eds.), *Research on technological innovation, management and policy*, Vol. 6: 89–153. Stamford, CT: JAI Press.

Burgelman, R. A., Floyd, S. W., Laamanen, T. et al. 2018. Strategy processes and practices: Dialogues and intersections. *Strategic Management Journal*, 39(3): 531–558.

Burgelman, R. A., & Grove, A. S. 1996. Strategic dissonance. *California Management Review*, 38(2): 8–28.

Burgelman, R. A., & Grove, A. S. 2007. Let chaos reign, then rein in chaos-repeatedly: Managing strategic dynamics for corporate longevity. *Strategic Management Journal*, 28(10): 965–979.

Burgelman, R. A., McKinney, W., & Meza, P. E. 2017. *Becoming Hewlett Packard: Why strategic leadership matters.* New York: Oxford University Press.

Burgelman, R. A., & Mittman, B. S. 1994. An intraorganizational ecological perspective on managerial risk behavior. In J. A. C. Baum, & J. V. Singh (Eds.), *Evolutionary dynamics of organizations*: 53–75. New York: Oxford University Press.

Burgelman, R. A., & Singh, J. V. 1987. Strategy and organization: An evolutionary approach. *Academy of Management Annual Meeting*. New Orleans, LA.

Burgelman, R. A., Snihur, Y., & Thomas, L. D. W. 2022a. Adapting to an evolving ecosystem: How ecosystem awareness and resource allocation drive CEO strategizing. Working Paper.

Burgelman, R. A., Snihur, Y., & Thomas, L. D. W. 2022b. Why multibusiness corporations split: CEO strategizing as the ecosystem evolves. *Journal of Management*, 48(7): 2108–2151.

Burgelman, R. A., & Sridharan, A. 2021. A process model of corporate venture capital as external innovation capability: The case of JetBlue Technology Ventures. Stanford Research Paper Series 3962, Stanford Business School.

Burt, R. S. 1992. *Structural holes*. Cambridge, MA: Harvard University Press.

Camerer, C. F. 1991. Does strategy research need game theory? *Strategic Management Journal*, 12: 137–152.

Campbell, D. T. 1965. Variation and selective retention in socio-cultural evolution. In H. R. Barringer, G. I. Blanksten, & R. W. Mack (Eds.), *Social change in developing areas: A reinterpretation of evolutionary theory*: 19–49. Cambridge, MA: Schenkman.

Cao, Q., Maruping, L. M., & Takeuchi, R. 2006. Disentangling the effects of CEO turnover and succession on organizational capabilities: A social network perspective. *Organization Science*, 17(5): 563–576.

Carpenter, M. A., Geletkanycz, M. A., & Sanders, W. G. 2004. Upper echelons research revisited: Antecedents, elements, and consequences of top management team composition. *Journal of Management*, 30(6): 749–778.

Chandler, A. D. 1962. *Strategy and structure: Chapters in the history of the American industrial enterprise*. Cambridge, MA: MIT Press.

Chatterjee, A., & Hambrick, D. C. 2007. It's all about me: Narcissistic chief executive officers and their effects on company strategy and performance. *Administrative Science Quarterly*, 52(3): 351–386.

Chatterjee, A., & Hambrick, D. C. 2011. Executive personality, capability cues, and risk taking: How narcissistic CEOs react to their successes and stumbles. *Administrative Science Quarterly*, 56(2): 202–237.

Chesbrough, H. W., & Appleyard, M. M. 2007. Open innovation and strategy. *California Management Review*, 50(1): 57–76.

Chesbrough, H. W., & Rosenbloom, R. S. 2002. The role of the business model in capturing value from innovation: Evidence from Xerox corporation's technology spin-off companies. *Industrial and Corporate Change*, 11(3): 529–555.

Cho, T. S., & Hambrick, D. C. 2006. Attention as the mediator between top management team characteristics and strategic change: The case of airline deregulation. *Organization Science*, 17(4): 453–469.

Christensen, C. M. 1997. *The innovator's dilemma: When new technologies cause great firms to fail*. Boston, MA: Harvard Business School Press.

Christensen, C. M., Raynor, M. E., & McDonald, R. 2015. What is disruptive innovation? *Harvard Business Review*, 93(12): 44–53.

Christensen, C. M., & Rosenbloom, R. S. 1995. Explaining the attacker's advantage: Technological paradigms, organizational dynamics, and the value network. *Research Policy*, 24(2): 233–257.

Clark, K. B., & Wheelwright, S. C. 1993. *Managing new product and process development: Text and cases*. New York: The Free Press.

Cohen, L. E., & Machalek, R. 1988. A general theory of expropriative crime: An evolutionary ecological approach. *American Journal of Sociology*, 94(3): 465–501.

Cozzolino, A., & Verona, G. in press. Responding to complementary-asset discontinuities: A multilevel adaptation framework of resources, demand, and ecosystems. *Organization Science*.

Crossland, C., Zyung, J., Hiller, N. J., & Hambrick, D. C. 2013. CEO career variety: Effects on firm-level strategic and social novelty. *Academy of Management Journal*, 57(3): 652–674.

Das, T. K. 2004. Strategy and time: Really recognizing the future. In H. Tsoukas, & J. Shepherd (Eds.), *Managing the future: Foresight in the knowledge economy*: 58–74. Oxford: Blackwell.

Dattée, B., Alexy, O., & Autio, E. 2018. Maneuvering in poor visibility: How firms play the ecosystem game when uncertainty is high. *Academy of Management Journal*, 61(2): 466–498.

David, P. A. 1985. Clio and the economics of qwerty. *The American Economic Review*, 75(2): 332–337.

Dawkins, R. 1986. *The blind watchmaker*. New York: Norton.

Ethiraj, S. K., & Levinthal, D. 2004. Modularity and innovation in complex systems. *Management Science*, 50: 159–173.

Feldman, E. R. 2014. Legacy divestitures: Motives and implications. *Organization Science*, 25(3): 815–832.

Firestein, S. 2016. *Failure: Why science is so successful*. Oxford: Oxford University Press.

Freeman, J., Carroll, G. R., & Hannan, M. T. 1983. The liability of newness: Age dependence in organizational death rates. *American Sociological Review*, 48(5): 692–710.

Gaddis, J. L. 2002. *The landscape of history: How historians map the past.* New York: Oxford University Press.

Galbraith, J. K. 1967. *The new industrial state.* Boston, MA: Houghton Mifflin.

Galunic, D. C., & Weeks, J. R. 2017. Intraorganizational ecology. In J. A. C. Baum (Ed.), *The Blackwell companion to organizations*, 75–97. Oxford: Blackwell.

Garnsey, E., Lorenzoni, G., & Ferriani, S. 2008. Speciation through entrepreneurial spin-off: The Acorn-ARM story. *Research Policy*, 37(2): 210–224.

Garud, R., & Karnoe, P. 2001. Path creation as a process of mindful deviation. In R. Garud, & P. Karnoe (Eds.), *Path dependence and creation*: 1–38. Mahwah, NJ: Lawrence Erlbaum Associates.

Garud, R., Kumaraswamy, A., & Karnøe, P. 2010. Path dependence or path creation? *Journal of Management Studies*, 47(4): 760–774.

Garud, R., Kumaraswamy, A., Roberts, A., & Xu, L. 2022. Liminal movement by digital platform-based sharing economy ventures: The case of Uber Technologies. *Strategic Management Journal*, 43(3): 447–475.

Gawer, A. 2014. Bridging differing perspectives on technological platforms: Toward an integrative framework. *Research Policy*, 43(7): 1239–1249.

Gersick, C. J. G. 1991. Revolutionary change theories: A multilevel exploration of the punctuated equilibrium paradigm. *Academy of Management Review*, 16(1): 10–36.

Gerstner, W.-C., König, A., Enders, A., & Hambrick, D. C. 2013. CEO narcissism, audience engagement, and organizational adoption of technological discontinuities. *Administrative Science Quarterly*, 58(2): 257–291.

Ghemawat, P. 1991. *Commitment: The dynamic of strategy.* New York: The Free Press.

Gilbert, C. G. 2005. Unbundling the structure of inertia: Resource versus routine rigidity. *Academy of Management Journal*, 48(5): 741–763.

Gilbert, C. G. 2006. Change in the presence of residual fit: Can competing frames coexist? *Organization Science*, 17(1): 150–167.

Glaser, B. G., & Strauss, A. L. 1967. *The discovery of grounded theory: Strategies for qualitative research.* New York: Aldine de Gruyter.

Gray, B., Purdy, J. M., & Ansari, S. 2015. From interactions to institutions: Microprocesses of framing and mechanisms for the structuring of institutional fields. *Academy of Management Review*, 40(1): 115–143.

Grinyer, P., & McKiernan, P. 1990. Generating major change in stagnating companies. *Strategic Management Journal*, 11: 131–146.

Hambrick, D. C. 2007. Upper echelons theory: An update. *Academy of Management Review*, 32(2): 334–343.

Hambrick, D. C., & Mason, P. A. 1984. Upper echelons: The organization as a reflection of its top managers. *Academy of Management Review*, 9(2): 193–206.

Hannan, M. T., & Freeman, J. 1977. The population ecology of organizations. *American Journal of Sociology*, 82(5): 929–964.

Hannan, M. T., & Freeman, J. 1984. Structural inertia and organizational change. *American Sociological Review*, 49(2): 149–164.

Hatch, M. J., & Schultz, M. 2017. Toward a theory of using history authentically: Historicizing in the Carlsberg Group. *Administrative Science Quarterly*, 62(4): 657–697.

Helfat, C. E., & Martin, J. A. 2015. Dynamic managerial capabilities. *Journal of Management*, 41(5): 1281–1312.

Helfat, C. E., & Peteraf, M. A. 2015. Managerial cognitive capabilities and the microfoundations of dynamic capabilities. *Strategic Management Journal*, 36(6): 831–850.

Helfat, C. E., & Raubitschek, R. S. 2018. Dynamic and integrative capabilities for profiting from innovation in digital platform-based ecosystems. *Research Policy*, 47(8): 1391–1399.

Henderson, A. D., Miller, D., & Hambrick, D. C. 2006. How quickly do CEOs become obsolete? Industry dynamism, CEO tenure, and company performance. *Strategic Management Journal*, 27(5): 447–460.

Hou, H., Cui, Z., & Shi, Y. 2020. Learning club, home court, and magnetic field: Facilitating business model portfolio extension with a multi-faceted corporate ecosystem. *Long Range Planning*, 53(4): 101970.

Hutt, M. D., Reingen, P. H., & Ronchetto, J. R. 1988. Tracing emergent processes in marketing strategy formation. *Journal of Marketing*, 52(1): 4–19.

Isaacson, W. 2011. *Steve Jobs*. New York: Simon & Schuster.

Iyer, B. R., & Basole, R. C. 2016. Visualization to understand ecosystems. *Communications of the ACM*, 59(11): 27–30.

Jacobides, M. G., Brusoni, S., & Candelon, F. 2021. The evolutionary dynamics of the artificial intelligence ecosystem. *Strategy Science*, 6(4): 412–435.

Jacobides, M. G., Cennamo, C., & Gawer, A. 2018. Towards a theory of ecosystems. *Strategic Management Journal*, 39(8): 2255–2276.

Joshi, A., Hambrick, D. C., & Kang, J. 2021. The generativity mindsets of chief executive officers: a new perspective on succession outcomes. *Academy of Management Review*, 46(2): 385–405.

Kagono, T., Nonaka, I., Sakakibara, K., & Okumura, A. 1985. *Strategic vs evolutionary management: A US–Japan comparison of strategy and organization*. New York: North-Holland.

Kahneman, D., Sibony, O., & Sunstein, C. R. 2021. *Noise: A flaw in human judgment*. New York: Little, Brown Spark.

Kaplan, S. 2008. Cognition, capabilities, and incentives: Assessing firm response to the fiber-optic revolution. *Academy of Management Journal*, 51(4): 672–695.

Kaplan, S., & Orlikowski, W. J. 2013. Temporal work in strategy making. *Organization Science*, 24(4): 965–995.

Kapoor, R., & Lee, J. M. 2013. Coordinating and competing in ecosystems: How organizational forms shape new technology investments. *Strategic Management Journal*, 34(3): 274–296.

Karim, S., & Capron, L. 2016. Reconfiguration: Adding, redeploying, recombining and divesting resources and business units. *Strategic Management Journal*, 37(13): E54–E62.

Keil, T., McGrath, R. G., & Tukiainen, T. 2009. Gems from the ashes: Capability creation and transformation in internal corporate venturing. *Organization Science*, 20(3): 601–620.

Kesner, I. F., & Sebora, T. C. 1994. Executive succession: Past, present & future. *Journal of Management*, 20(2), 327–372.

Khanagha, S., Volberda, H., & Oshri, I. 2014. Business model renewal and ambidexterity: Structural alteration and strategy formation process during transition to a cloud business model. *R&D Management*, 44(3): 322–340.

Kissinger, H., Schmidt, E., & Huttenlocher, D. 2021. *The age of AI*. New York: Little, Brown.

Klingebiel, R., & Rammer, C. 2014. Resource allocation strategy for innovation portfolio management. *Strategic Management Journal*, 35(2): 246–268.

Kouamé, S., & Langley, A. 2018. Relating microprocesses to macro-outcomes in qualitative strategy process and practice research. *Strategic Management Journal*, 39(3): 559–581.

Kraatz, M. S., & Moore, J. H. 2002. Executive migration and institutional change. *Academy of Management Journal*, 45(1): 120–143.

Lanzolla, G., & Markides, C. 2021. A business model view of strategy. *Journal of Management Studies*, 58(2), 540–553.

Larson, E. J. 2021. *The myth of artificial intelligence: Why computers can't think the way we do*. Cambridge, MA: The Belknap Press of Harvard University Press.

Leonard-Barton, D. 1990. A dual methodology for case studies: Synergistic use of a longitudinal single site with replicated multiple sites. *Organization Science*, 1(3): 248–266.

Leppänen, P., George, G., & Alexy, O. in press. When do novel business models lead to high firm performance? A configurational approach to value drivers, competitive strategy, and firm environment. *Academy of Management Journal.*

Levinthal, D. A. 1991. Organizational adaptation and environmental selection-interrelated processes of change. *Organization Science*, 2(1): 140–145.

Levinthal, D. A. 2017. Resource allocation and firm boundaries. *Journal of Management*, 43(8): 2580–2587.

Levinthal, D. A. 2021. *Evolutionary processes and organizational adaptation: A mendelian perspective on strategic management.* Oxford: Oxford University Press.

Levinthal, D. A., & March, J. G. 1993. The myopia of learning. *Strategic Management Journal*, 14(Special Issue): 95–112.

Lovas, B., & Ghoshal, S. 2000. Strategy as guided evolution. *Strategic Management Journal*, 21(9): 875–896.

Lumsden, C. J., & Singh, J. V. 1990. The dynamics of organizational speciation. In V. Singh Jitendra (Ed.), *Organizational evolution: New directions*: 145–163. London: Sage.

Mantere, S. 2008. Role expectations and middle manager strategic agency. *Journal of Management Studies*, 45(2): 294–316.

Mantovani, A., & Ruiz-Aliseda, F. 2016. Equilibrium innovation ecosystems: The dark side of collaborating with complementors. *Management Science*, 62(2): 534–549.

Marston, S., Li, Z., Bandyopadhyay, S., Zhang, J., & Ghalsasi, A. 2011. Cloud computing—The business perspective. *Decision Support Systems*, 51(1): 176–189.

Maritan, C. A., & Lee, G. K. 2017. Bringing a resource and capability lens to resource allocation. *Journal of Management*, 43(8): 2609–2619.

Martins, L. L., Rindova, V. P., & Greenbaum, B. E. 2015. Unlocking the hidden value of concepts: A cognitive approach to business model innovation. *Strategic Entrepreneurship Journal*, 9(1): 99–117.

Massa, L., Tucci, C. L., & Afuah, A. 2017. A critical assessment of business model research. *Academy of Management Annals*, 11(1): 73–104.

McDonald, R. M., & Eisenhardt, K. M. 2020. Parallel play: Startups, nascent markets, and effective business-model design. *Administrative Science Quarterly*, 65(2): 483–523.

Menz, M., & Scheef, C. 2014. Chief strategy officers: Contingency analysis of their presence in top management teams. *Strategic Management Journal*, 35(3): 461–471.

Merton, R. K. 1957. *Social theory and social structure.* Glencoe, IL: The Free Press.

Mintzberg, H. 1978. Patterns in strategy formation. *Management Science*, 24(9): 934–948.

Mintzberg, H., Ahlstrand, B., & Lampel, J. 1998. *Strategy safari: A guided tour through the wilds of strategic management*. New York: The Free Press.

Mintzberg, H., & Waters, J. A. 1985. Of strategies, deliberate and emergent. *Strategic Management Journal*, 6: 257–272.

Mirabeau, L., & Maguire, S. 2014. From autonomous strategic behavior to emergent strategy. *Strategic Management Journal*, 35(8): 1202–1229.

Mizruchi, M. S., & Marshall, L. J. 2016. Corporate CEOs, 1890–2015: Titans, bureaucrats, and saviors. *Annual Review of Sociology*, 42(1): 143–163.

Nadkarni, S., & Chen, J. 2014. Bridging yesterday, today, and tomorrow: CEO temporal focus, environmental dynamism, and rate of new product introduction. *Academy of Management Journal*, 57(6): 1810–1833.

Nelson, R. R., & Winter, S. G. 1982. *An evolutionary theory of economic change*. Cambridge, MA: Harvard University Press.

O'Reilly, C. A., & Tushman, M. L. 2011. Organizational ambidexterity in action: How managers explore and exploit. *California Management Review*, 53(4): 5–22.

Ojanperä, T., & Vuori, T. O. 2021. *Platform strategy: Transform your business with AI, platforms and human intelligence*. London: Kogan Page.

Paret, P. 1986. *Makers of modern strategy*. Princeton, NJ: Princeton University Press.

Penrose, E. 1959. *The theory of the growth of the firm*. Oxford: Oxford University Press.

Pettigrew, A. M. 1990. Longitudinal field research on change: Theory and practice. *Organization Science*, 1(3): 267–292.

Pfeffer, J., & Salancik, G. R. 1978. *The external control of organizations*. New York: Harper & Row.

Pollock, T. G., & Rindova, V. P. 2003. Media legitimation effects in the market for initial public offerings. *Academy of Management Journal*, 46(5): 631–642.

Porter, M. E. 1980. *Competitive strategy: Techniques for analyzing industries and competitors*. New York: The Free Press.

Pratap, S., & Saha, B. 2018. Evolving efficacy of managerial capital, contesting managerial practices, and the process of strategic renewal. *Strategic Management Journal*, 39(3): 759–793.

Prigogine, I. 1980. *From being to becoming: Time and complexity in the physical sciences*. New York: WH Freeman.

Quinn, J.B. 1980. *Strategies for change: Logical incrementalism*. Homewoood, Ill.: Irwin

Quinn, J. B. 1989. Strategic change: "Logical incrementalism." *MIT Sloan Management Review*, 30(4): 45–60.

Raisch, S., & Birkinshaw, J. 2008. Organizational ambidexterity: Antecedents, outcomes, and moderators. *Journal of Management*, 34(3): 375–409.

Rao, H. 1994. The social construction of reputation: Certification contests, legitimation, and the survival of organizations in the American automobile industry: 1895–1912. *Strategic Management Journal*, 15(S1): 29–44.

Ravasi, D., Rindova, V. P., & Stigliani, I. 2019. The stuff of legend: History, memory and the temporality of organizational identity construction. *Academy of Management Journal*, 62(5): 1523–1555.

Ries, E. 2011. *The lean startup: How today's entrepreneurs use continuous innovation to create radically successful businesses*. New York: Crown Business.

Romanelli, E., & Tushman, M. L. 1994. Organizational transformation as punctuated equilibrium: An empirical-test. *Academy of Management Journal*, 37(5): 1141–1166.

Rumelt, R. P., Schendel, D., & Teece, D. J. 1994. *Fundamental issues in strategy: A research agenda*. Boston, MA: Harvard Business School Press.

Sabatier, V., Mangematin, V., & Rousselle, T. 2010. From recipe to dinner: Business model portfolios in the European biopharmaceutical industry. *Long Range Planning*, 43(2): 431–447.

Sahal, D. 1979. A unified theory of self-organization. *Journal of Cybernetics*, 9(2): 127–142.

Saloner, G. 1991. Modeling, game theory, and strategic management. *Strategic Management Journal*, 12: 119–136.

Sayles, L. R. 1965. *Managerial behavior; administration in complex organizations*. New York: McGraw-Hill.

Schelling, T. C. 1963. *The strategy of conflict*. Cambridge, MA: Harvard University Press.

Schreieck, M., Wiesche, M., & Krcmar, H. 2021. Capabilities for value co-creation and value capture in emergent platform ecosystems: A longitudinal case study of SAP's cloud platform. *Journal of Information Technology*, 36(4): 365–390.

Selznick, P. 1957. *Leadership in administration*. New York: Harper & Row.

Shipilov, A., & Gawer, A. 2020. Integrating research on interorganizational networks and ecosystems. *Academy of Management Annals*, 14(1): 92–121.

Simon, H. A. 1962. The architecture of complexity. *Proceedings of American Philosophy Society*, 106(6): 467–482.

Simsek, Z. 2009. Organizational ambidexterity: Towards a multilevel understanding. *Journal of Management Studies*, 46(4): 597–624.

Singh, J. V., & Lumsden, C. J. 1990. Theory and research in organizational ecology. *Annual Review of Sociology*, 16(1): 161–195.

Singh, J. V., Tucker, D. J., & House, R. J. 1986. Organizational legitimacy and the liability of newness. *Administrative Science Quarterly*, 31(2): 171–193.

Snihur, Y., & Bocken, N. 2022. A call for action: The impact of business model innovation on business ecosystems, society and planet. *Long Range Planning*: 102182.

Snihur, Y., & Eisenhardt, K. M. 2022. Looking forward, looking back: Strategic organization and the business model concept. *Strategic Organization*, 20(4), 757–770.

Snihur, Y., & Tarzijan, J. 2018. Managing complexity in a multi-business-model organization. *Long Range Planning*, 51(1): 50–63.

Snihur, Y., Thomas, L. D. W., & Burgelman, R. A. 2018. An ecosystem-level process model of business model disruption: The disruptor's gambit. *Journal of Management Studies*, 55(7): 1278–1316.

Snihur, Y., Thomas, L. D., & Burgelman, R. A. 2022. Strategically Managing the Business Model Portfolio Trajectory. *California Management Review*, 00081256221140930.

Snihur, Y., & Zott, C. 2020. The genesis and metamorphosis of novelty imprints: How business model innovation emerges in young ventures. *Academy of Management Journal*, 63(2): 554–583.

Snihur, Y., Zott, C., & Amit, R. 2021. Managing the value appropriation dilemma in business model innovation. *Strategy Science*, 6(1): 22–38.

Spender, J., & Kraaijenbrink, J. 2011. Why competitive strategy succeeds-and with whom. In R. Huggins, & H. Izushi (Eds.), *Competition, competitive advantage, and clusters: The ideas of Michael Porter*: 33–55. Oxford: Oxford University Press.

Steffensen, D. S., Ellen, B. P., Wang, G., & Ferris, G. R. 2019. Putting the "management" back in human resource management: A review and agenda for future research. *Journal of Management*, 45(6): 2387–2418.

Stinchcombe, A. L. 1965. Social structure and organizations. In J. G. March (Ed.), *Handbook of organizations*: 142–193. Chicago, IL: Rand McNally.

Strogatz, S. H. 1994. *Nonlinear dynamics and chaos: With applications to physics, biology, chemistry, and engineering*. Reading, MA: Addison-Wesley.

Teece, D. J. 2007. Explicating dynamic capabilities: The nature and micro-foundations of (sustainable) enterprise performance. *Strategic Management Journal*, 28(13): 1319–1350.

Teece, D. J. 2010. Business models, business strategy and innovation. *Long Range Planning*, 43(2–3): 172–194.

Thiétart, R. A., & Forgues, B. 1995. Chaos theory and organization. *Organization Science*, 6(1): 19–31.

Thomas, L. D. W., & Autio, E. 2020. Innovation Ecosystems in Management: An Organizing Typology. In Michael A. Hitt (Ed.): Oxford Research Encyclopedia of Business and Management. Oxford, UK: Oxford University Press. DOI: 10.1093/acrefore/9780190224851.013.203.

Thomas, L. D. W., Autio, E., & Gann, D. M. 2022. Processes of ecosystem emergence. *Technovation*, 115, 102441.

Thomas, L. D. W., & Ritala, P. 2022. Ecosystem legitimacy emergence: A collective action view. *Journal of Management*, 48(3): 515–541.

Tolstoy, L. 1978. *War and peace*. London: Penguin Books.

Tsoukas, H., & Chia, R. 2002. On organizational becoming: Rethinking organizational change. *Organization Science*, 13(5): 567–582.

Tushman, M. L., & O'Reilly, C. A. 1997. *Winning through innovation: A practical guide to leading organizational change and renewal*. Boston, MA: Harvard Business Press.

Tushman, M. L., & Romanelli, E. 1985. Organizational evolution: A metamorphosis model of convergence and reorientation. *Research in Organizational Behavior*, 7: 171–222. Greenwich, CT: JAI Press.

Vaara, E., & Lamberg, J.-A. 2016. Taking historical embeddedness seriously: Three historical approaches to advance strategy process and practice research. *Academy of Management Review*, 41(4): 633–657.

Virany, B., Tushman, M. L., & Romanelli, E. 1992. Executive succession and organization outcomes in turbulent environments: An organization learning approach. *Organization Science*, 3(1): 72–91.

Wareham, J., Fox, P. B., & Cano Giner, J. L. 2014. Technology ecosystem governance. *Organization Science*, 25(4): 1195–1215.

Weick, K. E. 1979. *The social psychology of organizing*. Reading, MA: Addison-Wesley.

Weick, K. E., & Quinn, R. E. 1999. Organizational change and development. *Annual Review of Psychology*, 50(1): 361–386.

Winter, S. G. 1987. Knowledge and competence as strategic assets. In D. J. Teece (Ed.), *The competitive challenge: Strategies for industrial innovation and renewal*: 159–184. Cambridge, MA: Ballinger.

Wooldridge, B., Schmid, T., & Floyd, S. W. 2008. The middle management perspective on strategy process: Contributions, synthesis, and future research. *Journal of Management*, 34(6): 1190–1221.

Yadav, M. S., Prabhu, J. C., & Chandy, R. K. 2007. Managing the future: CEO attention and innovation outcomes. *Journal of Marketing*, 71(4): 84–101.

Yin, R. K. 2018. *Case study research and applications: Design and methods* (6th ed.). Beverley Hills, CA: Sage.

Zott, C., Amit, R., & Massa, L. 2011. The business model: recent developments and future research. *Journal of Management*, 37(4): 1019–1042.

Zuzul, T., & Tripsas, M. 2020. Start-up inertia versus flexibility: The role of founder identity in a nascent industry. *Administrative Science Quarterly*, 65(2): 395–433.

Acknowledgments

We would like to thank Tomi Laamanen, J. -C. Spender, and Tom Neuhauser for helpful comments on the early manuscript draft.

We dedicate this Element to our families and significant others.

Cambridge Elements ≡

Business Strategy

J.-C. Spender
Kozminski University

J.-C. Spender is a research Professor, Kozminski University. He has been active in the business strategy field since 1971 and is the author or co-author of 7 books and numerous papers. His principal academic interest is in knowledge-based theories of the private sector firm, and managing them.

Advisory Board

About the Series

Business strategy's reach is vast, and important too since wherever there is business activity there is strategizing. As a field, strategy has a long history from medieval and colonial times to today's developed and developing economies. This series offers a place for interesting and illuminating research including industry and corporate studies, strategizing in service industries, the arts, the public sector, and the new forms of Internet-based commerce. It also covers today's expanding gamut of analytic techniques.

Cambridge Elements ☰

Business Strategy

Elements in the Series

Printed in the United States
by Baker & Taylor Publisher Services